The 3 Cords of Apostolic Leadership

The 3 Cords of Apostolic Leadership

A leader's guide to effectual growth

Amy Olson and Chris Olson

ISBN: 1946912026
ISBN 13: 9781946912022
Library of Congress Control Number: 2017905898
Amy Olson, Creedmoor North Carolina

Dedication

In Honor, and loving memory, of those great apostolic leaders that have gone before us leaving a foundation and legacy for our future generations. In particular those that had the biggest impact in our lives:

Our grandparents, A.L. (1933-2016)
and June Durand (1937-1994)
Our Bishop, G.A. (1919-2010) and Vesta Mangun

And

To all of our family and friends, with love...

Acknowledgements

FIRST AND FOREMOST to our one true living God, Jesus Christ— The very reason we exist. Thank you for everything–salvation, love, and the opportunity to worship you. May our lives bring you glory and honor!

To our pastors Rev. David Akers, Rev. Dennis Durand, and Rev. Anthony Mangun and their families—Thank you for the wisdom, guidance, patience, and love that you impart to us. You have been the epitome of leadership in our lives and to you we are forever grateful.

To all of our professors and the staff at Regent University's School of Business and Leadership, in particular our dissertation chairs and leaders, Dr. Bruce Winston, Dr. Doris Gomez, Dr. Kathleen Patterson, and Dr. Diane Wiater—Thank you for the knowledge, advice, and encouragement throughout this journey.

Endorsements

"JOHN MAXWELL ONCE observed, "Everything rises and falls on leadership." I might paraphrase that specific to pastors and say, "In the local church, everything rises and falls on spiritual leadership." This work can help each pastor personally assess and take steps to develop his own personal spiritual leadership quotient. It can also be a tool for that pastor to use with his congregational leaders, assisting them in developing themselves as spiritual men and women in service to the Kingdom of God. Whether in a metropolitan area or rural community, whether with a congregation of a few or many, *The 3 Cords of Apostolic Leadership* will be an invaluable asset to personal and group leadership development in any church regardless of size or location."

~ **ANTHONY MANGUN**, Senior Pastor - *The Pentecostals of Alexandria*
  Alexandria, Louisiana

"It is my delight to introduce to you Chris and Amy Olson. They bring to the Apostolic table a diverse and much needed viewpoint of leadership and leadership training. I believe you will be enriched and certainly enlightened by this much needed and very timely book. You will recognize the great effort and energy expended to make this resource available to you and your leaders. Thank you Amy and Chris for your investment and insight to the Kingdom of God."

~ **DAVID W. AKERS,** Pastor – *Covenant Life*
Butner, North Carolina

"It is increasingly clear that the need for competent leadership in the church is essential. The 3 Cords of Apostolic Leadership defines organizational leadership accurately, practically, and according to Scriptures. It is replete with key leadership principles and helpful ideas on how to implement these principles in a realistic and meaningful way. Ministers and laity alike will find this work helpful in their endeavors to hone their abilities, their talents, and their competences for this all-important calling - to be a church leader."

~ **VESTA MANGUN** - *The Pentecostals of Alexandria*
Alexandria, Louisiana

Table of Contents

Preface

WE ARE THRILLED that you have chosen this study and are as passionate about developing leaders within your church as we are! For many seasoned leaders and pastors, the concept of developing leaders may seem elementary or common sense as it is vital to produce church growth. In fact, a recent study that we conducted surveying apostolic churches reveals that all respondents felt leadership development was important.[1] However, many churches do not have a formal leadership development program. There are many viable reasons as to why this may be, and we are not condemning those that do not have such training. On the other hand, some churches have informal mentoring or other ministry training in which leadership concepts are incorporated. To complicate things, there are very few apostolic or even Christian resources available on the topic, and those that do exist are mainly books.

Thus, this resource was crafted to aid in the leadership development process, providing a tool to help grow leaders within your church or organization. It is purposely structured not to be a comprehensive resource, but designed with the capability to tailor toward your individual and organizational needs, covering many of the vital areas of leadership. Some of these concepts are often taken for granted by experienced church leaders as something that is just understood or expected of all, particularly if they have been saved and are striving to live by the Word. The principles identified in this study are founded upon leadership theory, best practices, and the Word of God.

To clarify, this is not a minister development program but is focused on leadership development, which can certainly coincide with minister development. In fact, we strongly recommend adding it alongside any ministry development efforts. However, it can also be used as an independent resource to develop any person interested in improving their leadership skills both within and outside of the church. If you think about it, many saints come from a workplace environment where they are consistently told what to do and how to do it and often do not have an opportunity to develop these skills. They then come to church where they are in charge of teaching classes, leading music, or sometimes running departments. This is a great resource for those people. It is also a great study tool for the seasoned leader to remind us all that we are called. We have a higher purpose that requires a higher standard to lead the people of God closer to Him.

This is truly our desire and motive behind this material, to fulfill the purpose of Christ for our calling and to provide study material that will aid in developing vital leadership traits. We are servants of the King of Kings and Lord of Lords, just as you are students of the Word of God. We have spent the last several years of our lives studying leadership at a graduate level in a Christian college, Regent University. We have also been in leadership for more than twenty-five years within the church as well as in business organizations. We have held ministry positions in start-ups, home mission churches, as well as churches with thousands in attendance. In these capacities, we have held several positions, including assistant pastors (unofficially), youth leaders, college and career directors, music leaders, Sunday school teachers, home Bible study teachers, and other service ministries that come naturally for those in ministry, such as cleaning the church, feeding the poor, ministering to the sick and those in need, or whatever the Lord asks of us.

The fact that we are not pastors gives us a unique perspective in that we know and understand what it is to be in ministry roles under that authority of God and pastor. However, we have served alongside pastors, assisting them in every aspect of ministry, including officiating church services, and have been raised in a pastor's home, so we also know firsthand the requirements of that role.

The pastor who is attuned with God will know what is best for His Church and will have the capability to tailor this resource to assist with developing church leaders and meeting the needs of that specific church. While there are probably many more qualified people, our goal is to humbly share our passion, knowledge, and what we feel the Lord has called us to do for His Kingdom. We have prayed and fasted over this project as well as sought guidance from our leaders for many years. Our hope and prayer is that people will be developed, and strong leaders will emerge to propagate the gospel. We are not talking about people who are just looking for a title, but those who truly want to serve the Master and *lead* others to Him. We have learned over the years that some of the best leaders and people you will ever meet are those without a formal title. They live by example in their humility and work they do for the Lord.

Structure of This Study

The structure of this program is based on the analogy of a three-fold cord found in the scripture: "a threefold cord is not quickly broken" (Ecclesiastes 4:12). The three-fold cord includes (1) spiritual formation, (2) leadership competencies, and (3) church and organizational development.

"A threefold cord is not quickly broken" (Ecclesiastes 4:12)

The cords can also be viewed as separate modules.

(Cord 1) Spiritual Formation: In this module, we take a look at the vital spiritual disciplines that are crucial and foundational to apostolic leadership development. The topics covered are Prayer, Fasting, Bible Study, Spiritual Gifts, Fruits of the Spirit, and The Empowerment of the Holy Ghost in a Leader's Life.

(Cord 2) Leadership Competencies: In this module, we study several major leadership competencies. We define competencies as the basic behavior, knowledge, skills, and abilities essential to Christian leaders. These topics include concepts of Servant Leadership and Transformational Leadership. We introduce a model for Servant Leadership consisting of four main categories, including Love, Integrity, Discernment, and Stewardship. Each category has the following subcategories:

1. Love: humility, empathy, altruism, healing, and service
2. Integrity: authenticity, ethics, trust, and honor
3. Discernment: awareness, internal locus of control, listening, conceptualization, and foresight
4. Stewardship: growth, community, persuasion, and empowerment

For Transformational Leadership, we study the concepts of charisma, being visionary, and leading change. Additionally, we identify other important leadership characteristics such as communication, temperance, wisdom, and emotional, social, and cultural intelligence. Finally, we provide some strategies for self-development including the use of assessments and coaching.

(Cord 3) Organizational Development: This module explores leadership from an organizational perspective through the lens of scripture. Topics covered include: Strategic Leadership,

Organizational Culture, Innovation and Foresight, Outreach, Visitor Retention and Assimilation, Effectively Managing Conflict and Leading Change, Teamwork and Team Building, Pastoral Authority and Church Structure, Systems, Succession Planning, and Methods for leader development.

Finally, the appendix includes coaching techniques and how coaching can be incorporated in the church as well as three assessments: Servant Leadership, Transformational, and Communication.

This training material is designed to be taught in a group setting, targeting aspiring and experienced church leaders. However, it can also be done as an individual study. All scripture is King James Version unless otherwise noted. We reference *Strong's Concordance* for all Greek and Hebrew word meanings and online dictionaries such as *Webster* or dictionary.com for definitions. The term organization is used interchangeably with church, but can be interpreted in a broader sense, as the application of the curriculum applies to single and multiple entities as well as various sizes. Also, we often use the word "followers" as an interchangeable term to describe the people you lead. It is with the understanding that we all are followers of Christ and should be leading people to Him. Moreover, in 1 Corinthians 11:1 Paul states "Be ye followers of me, even as I also am of Christ."

Each module is meant to be interactive, thus we include activities, discussion questions, and assessments to aid in the learning process. Again, this material is not exhaustive, so we encourage teachers to bring their own expertise, knowledge of scripture, stories, videos, and experiences to supplement the teaching material, just as one would any other group study. The teacher can be a pastor or senior leader. If not the pastor, the teacher should have leadership experience and the capability to answer questions and act as a facilitator for growth. We recommend the teacher read an entire module first before formulating and structuring specific lessons, as many concepts overlap. We have structured the topics so that there is a nice flow; however, some people may prefer to discuss certain concepts together. This is particularly the case with the leadership competencies in the second module, such as love, empathy, and altruism. Additionally, topics may also be discussed in another module but from a different perspective. For example, vision is a competency that an individual must possess as well as having the ability to cast that vision for organizational growth.

Please visit our website at www.apostolicleader.org for a free facilitator's guide, assistance implementing this pro-gram, and other church leadership development information. The facilitator's guide provides teaching tips and instructions for all activities. We welcome feedback and comments, as we are always striving to better serve the Kingdom. Thank you once again for your service to Christ and allowing our study to aid in your leadership development endeavor.

---

1 Chris Olson, "ALJC Leadership Development Analysis" (master's thesis, Regent University, Virginia Beach, 2016).

Three-Fold Cord of Spiritual Leadership Development

CLOSE YOUR EYES and imagine a single stranded cord suspending a very heavy object in the air. As gravity pulls down on the object, the single piece of rope begins to break apart until the object falls and is lost. In Ecclesiastes 4:9–12, we see a powerful illustration of empowerment on an exponential level. The scripture begins with a description of how feeble one person is by himself. However, success is compounded when we add another entity. Two are certainly better than one. United, they work together to gain an increase in reward for their labor. They, together, help each other when hard times arise or when one of them falls in some sort of snare. They, jointly, can withstand any obstacle better than each one can alone. There is certainly an exponential increase in power when you begin to couple people, principles, resources, you name it. The synergy that this combined effect has creates a fortified structure that is stable, balanced, and very hard to bring down. After all, Moses wrote, "at the mouth of two witnesses, or at the mouth of three witnesses, shall the matter be established" (Deuteronomy 19:15).

This verse undoubtedly has to do with the law, but if we view this as only a letter, then we miss the entire spirit behind the words, and we become legalistic in our understanding. The Lord, through the Mosaic Law, was establishing a standard. That standard is the fact that only one voice, principle, and precept is not powerful enough to stand by itself. Both Jesus and Paul echo this principle in their teachings. Jesus, in Matthew 18:15–16, instructs us how to deal with unruly brethren through the combined synergy of two or three. Furthermore, Paul, in his second recorded letter to the Corinthian church, uses this principle to continue to preach to them about their own struggles (2 Corinthians 13:1). The point is that only one "witness" is not enough. Finally, Ecclesiastes tells us "a threefold cord is not quickly broken" (Ecclesiastes 4:12). A cord made up of three ropes is infinitely harder to break than its less fortified counterparts. Yes, two are better than one, but the structure gets much more rigid when you add a third dimension. To further illustrate, think of a three-legged stool. Without just one of its legs, it cannot stand, and it certainly cannot support anything.

This is the same for spiritual leadership in the apostolic church. Thus, this training material is founded on three areas of principle designed to "support" the ministry of our leaders, both seasoned and aspiring. Each cord has been verified and validated by extensive research so that every point made can most effectively lead you to a ministry that is successful in the Lord. The first cord that will be discussed is spiritual formation and development.

Spiritual Formation

CORD 1

Spiritual Formation

A MAJOR PART of any leader's routine is a process of continual learning. Ask any successful leader, and they will tell you that it is imperative for one to stay abreast of issues related to their field. This principle is equally important for church leaders, as they should strive to continually grow in the Lord. Those who profess a calling must also prepare for that calling and be diligent in spiritual formation and development. Remember, the burden of leadership is not a position of lofty estate, but it is the responsibility of being held accountable for the people you lead.

God has given us the responsibility of leadership. Many like to talk about the office, but they forget about or prove to be lackadaisical in the actual responsibility God imparts to His leaders. James 3:1 teaches us to, "be not many masters, knowing that we shall receive the greater condemnation." The word "masters" here comes from the Greek word *didaskalos,* meaning basically a teacher or instructor. It is the same word that John uses to describe the office of Nicodemus (John 3:10). What is interesting is Nicodemus, a spiritual leader of Israel, did not comprehend the things of God as far as the transitioning of spiritual dispensations. Ask him to interpret the Law, and he could probably quote it word for word, teach lessons on it, and exhaust himself while teaching all of its tedious details. But to know, disclose, and articulate the new and living way? Not so much. God wanted a transition, and His leaders of that day were aloof to that vision! God expects His leaders to be in tune with Him, having the mind of Christ. This in no way can happen without careful and diligent prayer, fasting, and Bible study. This is the only way to truly allow the gifts and fruits of the Spirit to work through you while being empowered by the Holy Ghost to be the leader that He has chosen you to be.

The issue of spiritual formation and development is imperative because those you lead will only go as far as you. The question is this: Would you want to be led by you? That is a pretty sobering question when you stop to ponder the implications. It causes us to think about our lifestyle, our habits, and the state and quality in which we exercise spiritual discipline. Simply, it means that we will never arrive at a point where we can stop being diligent in our own walk with God because, as a leader, you have more to care about than just yourself.

Chances are that if your pastor has identified you as a leader or potential leader, then you already have, to some degree, a level of spiritual discipline. You should already be attentive to prayer, fasting, Bible study, and other spiritual disciplines. However, the goal for this section is not just to teach that spiritual development is necessary, but also to instruct as to what it looks like in terms of church leadership. Let us not be indicted as being ignorant of God's plan because we have proven to be lazy in spiritual matters. The callings, gifts, lives, and souls of those you lead are left in your hands to mold. This is a massive responsibility and one that we should not take lightly. Thankfully, we share this responsibility with our pastors, who are ultimately charged with giving an account for everyone they lead. But nonetheless, you greatly affect those you lead for the good and also the bad. This is dictated largely by how faithful you are in prayer, fasting, and Bible study. We begin this section with a discussion on prayer, as it is the foundation for any ministry or position in the church.

CHAPTER 1

Prayer

THE CLICHÉS ARE many. Prayer is powerful, prayer is pivotal, prayer is paramount. While these are true, I am afraid that many, especially leaders in the church, fail to grasp the true meaning behind these words. God's leaders pray with fervor and passion. It is impossible to know exactly what the Lord sounded like when He prayed, but we can infer some things from the tonality and verbiage used in scripture.

There is no doubt that Jesus was a leader of leaders. While on earth, He prayed earnestly, with purpose and conviction. As God's leaders, we must pray with purpose, conviction, and fervor like never before. We have to intercede for those we lead, we have to pray earnestly for direction from God, and we must subdue our flesh lest we fall into temptation. Jesus prayed earnestly, so we could follow His lead. One of the most notable examples of this is the account of Jesus praying in the garden. Jesus, as a leader, had a responsibility to fulfill His purpose. He prayed earnestly to overcome the feelings with which "the cup" had burdened Him (Matthew 26:36–46; Mark 14:33–42; Luke 22:40–46). This instance alone is enough to change our prayer life forever if we allow it. For this foundational element of prayer, there are several crucial concepts that we wish to highlight, including earnest, watchful, and corporate prayer as demonstrated by Jesus in the garden just before His crucifixion. Additionally, sustainability through prayer, praying the Word, as well as praying in the Spirit are other vital components to a strong prayer life.

Earnest Prayer

The first point illustrates how earnest prayer is manifested. Matthew and Mark both make mention that Jesus went a little further. As leaders in the church, it is imperative that we go further in our prayers. "Patty cake" prayer that is only fit for the spiritual nursery does not move God! Fervent, heartfelt, earnest prayer is what God wants and expects, especially from His leaders. We cannot expect God to do great things if we don't have great prayer.

This kind of praying is the hallmark of all life-changing ministry. E.M. Bounds, the go-to source for everything prayer, said speaking to God for men is greater than speaking to men for God.[1] Prayer has always preceded great ministries: no prayer, no ministry, and little prayer, little ministry. In other words, the impact of our ministry is directly proportional to our prayer life. It is a one-to-one relationship. Without fervent and diligent prayer, it is impossible to be good stewards of the people and things God has placed in your charge. Fervent prayer is birthed through a life of dedicated discipline. Such leaders are not prone to making excuses that attempt to absolve them of this responsibility. Dedicated and disciplined prayer is their routine.

Now, when someone says that a certain action is a habit or part of a routine, we immediately begin to think that action does little to affect overall life because such things become disingenuous and automatic. However, that is simply not true. Just because something is a habit or custom does not mean that it is insincere. There are good habits and customs. Case in point: It was the Lord's custom to go to the synagogue (Luke 4:16). We can all agree that going to church faithfully is a good habit (Hebrews 10:25). We can also agree that Jesus was the most genuine person who ever walked the earth. Therefore, if Jesus had genuine and heartfelt customs of prayer and faithfulness to the house of God, then so can we.

Furthermore, with the birth of the church in the book of Acts comes the powerful words, "and they continued..." (Acts 2:42). They continued steadfastly, unshakable and unmovable in doctrine, fellowship, and most of all, prayers. We can have spiritually healthy habits. Rather than filling our time with mindless activities, we can spend our time wisely on the things that matter. The result will be a spiritually enriched life cultivated for proper leadership in the church. I am not trying to convince you to spend every waking moment in prayer. How would any other Kingdom work get done? God wants us to enjoy the life He has blessed us with, but we must live life with the proper priorities in place.

Watchful Prayer

For the second point, notice that when Jesus brought Peter, James, and John with Him, He told them not to simply join in prayer but to join in the "watch." Mark's account of this extraordinary and supernatural event pulls out one of the deeper, often hidden, meanings of prayer. The word "watch" in this scripture comes from the Greek word *gregoreo,* which means to be vigilant and awake. If we do not stay awake and vigilant in prayer, then the enemy will take us out of the presence and plan of God. Some may note that Jesus was actually the one who was taken away from the disciples. This perspective is absolutely correct, but let's think about this on a deeper level.

All of Christianity generally agrees that it was the ultimate plan of God for Jesus to be crucified (Revelation 13:8). But when the enemy came into the garden, the disciples scattered. In essence, they let the enemy confuse and convince them to run away from God's plan. They took themselves out of God's presence, all because they let the enemy come in through a lack of prayer and watchfulness! Let us not be ignorant of Satan's devices. Pray and earnestly seek the face of God that you may not fall into temptation and a snare. People are counting on your walk with God. Yes, they should have their eyes on Jesus, but as leaders in the church, we need to exemplify Him. It is true that we will never measure up to the full stature of Christ, but we can, through the power of prayer and the Spirit of God, strive to be like Him in all manner of behavior.

Vince Lombardi, the Hall of Fame head football coach for the Green Bay Packers, was quoted as saying, "Perfection is not attainable, but if we chase perfection then we can catch excellence." What a powerful statement. Because of the sinful nature of our flesh, we will never measure up to the perfection that is Jesus Christ, no matter how much we pray. So what, do we just stop praying because it's useless? Absolutely not! We use the fact that we are not perfect as a motivation to go deeper in prayer than we ever have. If we pursue the perfection of Jesus with all of our hearts, then we can catch excellence through the Holy Ghost.

Corporate Prayer

Lastly, and probably most importantly, Jesus showed us the importance of corporate prayer. All of the gospel accounts make specific mention of the Lord's command to watch except for John. In fact, Matthew, Mark, and Luke all give specific details about what transpired in the garden. However, John only mentions that Jesus led His disciples to that place. He then pens something powerful. He notes that Judas, on his way to betray Jesus, knew exactly where to find Him! Why? It's because He often went there with His disciples. Wow, what a testimony! Do we pray *with* those we lead and not just *for* them? They need to see us in earnest prayer before the throne of God. This fosters trust, love, respect, and accountability in the relationships that we have with them.

Jesus had such a prayer life that it was marked not only by His followers but also His enemies! If the enemy is going to find us, let him find us in prayer; in prayer for our pastor, in prayer for our church, and in prayer for those we lead! We have to show forth the example. Paul told both the Corinthian and Philippian churches to follow him because he was given to them as an example (1 Corinthians 11:1; Philippians 3:17). He did not make this statement in arrogance or a haughty spirit. He was simply stating the truth. Leaders are called and commissioned to take the lead. They are to be in the forefront so others can find the way.

Sustainability Through Prayer

Many leaders are only interested in coming up with the next big thing. They spend all of their time coming up with new programs and systems, but little time in prayer! What is perplexing to me is that all this time is spent on these "systems," but God does not anoint the synthetic. God has only and will only anoint men and women charged with His calling who have been engaged in prayer. From there, God anoints the system or program because the man or woman of God has been anointed.[2] It is true that leadership ideologies may allude to many systems and principles, but none of these things—no trait, no system, or any man-made thing—will ever be anointed of God unless that man or woman is first anointed. Only then can the tools, systems, and programs that they put in place become sustainably effective.

You cannot lead by traits alone. Such leadership actually cuts God out of the equation, because you lean more toward your own understanding instead of letting the Holy Ghost lead through you. This type of leadership entrusts too much of God's work to carnal things. What an egregious conflict of interest! The carnal mind focuses too much on natural things, which fights against God's laws and renders it incapable of discerning spiritual concepts (Romans 8:5–8; 1 Corinthians 2:14). Yes, God has given all of us certain gifts, talents, and traits that can aid in our leadership ability. But without prayer, none of these things will be sustainably effective. We have seen many church leaders who had amazing talents and abilities but lacked a prayer life. Sure, they may be successful for a time, but the end result is a ministry that falls flat and spins around in circles. It is not sustainable. This leads to frustration and eventually bitterness, all because prayer was absent from the leader's life! Everyone needs to be diligent in prayer, but especially God's leaders, for they help to propagate the gospel into this lost and dying world. But if there is no prayer, then there is no propagation.

It is a responsibility. A church leader cannot make it on intelligence alone. Paul was one of the most intelligent men of the old world, yet he still penned these powerful and inspiring words: "Pray without ceasing" (1 Thessalonians 5:17). God's leader prays continually. He or she lives their life with a spirit of prayer and faith. Without a prayer life, it is impossible to lead those God has entrusted to you. In fact, one can argue that if you are going to lead in the church, then you must spend more time in prayer than those you lead. Why? To boast about the time spent before the throne of God or to try to earn the position God has given you? Of course not! But as a leader, you are expected to lead. Leaders should go the extra mile in everything because that is what leaders do. They lead. They get out ahead of everyone else so they can build a bridge that will connect where they are to where God wants them to go.

⟡

Praying the Word

Additionally, there are two more points about prayer that are relevant for leadership and that pertain to a deeper prayer life, one that characterizes God's leaders. First, we should pray the Word of God. We learn this when we first learn how to pray, but this principle becomes infinitely more powerful when we understand it in the context of leadership. For example, knowing and reminding God that He said, "For I know the thoughts that I think toward you, saith the LORD, thoughts of peace, and not of evil, to give you an expected end," can really empower you to go boldly to the throne and intercede for someone who has fallen on hard times. Praying the Word of God helps us to connect with God and to speak boldly on their behalf because that is what leaders should do.

When we pray the Word of God, we are showing God that we trust wholeheartedly in His counsel and depend on it. The Word of God is so powerful that when spoken, things begin to happen in the spirit realm. Evil walls come crashing down, but godly walls are raised. Darkness fails, but the Light prevails. It is recommended that every leader use the Word of God as the sword of the Spirit for which it is designed. However, the ability to wield the sword of the Lord only comes with diligent study

(John 14:26). For more on that subject, please see the section on studying the Bible later in this module.

〜

Praying in the Spirit

Lastly, God's leaders should regularly pray in the Spirit. Being another sort of elementary aspect in the same vein as praying the Word, the power of praying in the Spirit from a leadership perspective is often lost in the battle for greater revelation. Often, leadership seeks that deeper edge so diligently, they forget that one of the most powerful things they can do is let the Spirit pray through them! We should all strive to develop a deeper understanding of the things of God and even God in general, but in so doing, let us not forget those rudimentary parts that make the machine of godly leadership so powerful. God has given us all the tools already; we just need to learn how to use them to our advantage in the office in which He has ordained us. Praying in the Spirit is powerful because it gives God the opportunity to speak through you.

There are many other things to say about prayer, but some are out of the scope of this study simply because if you are reading this material or sitting in a classroom setting focused on training church leaders, then you should at least have a decent prayer life. However, as a leader for God, the goal is to chase and pursue Him so when others follow, we don't lead them astray. Therefore, we should not be content at the place where our prayer life is now, but we should strive to build upon that prayer life to the point where we "hear" God leading us so we can effectively, successfully, and truly lead others.

Discussion Questions

1. Does the strength of your prayer life have any effect on your leadership ability? Explain.

2. Give some practical techniques that will bolster both the quality and quantity of your prayers.

3. Assuming that your motives and intentions are in the right place, explain the effect on your relationship with those you lead when they see you in prayer.

4. How can we learn to pray from observing the Lord's actions in scripture?

CHAPTER 2

Fasting

WE NOW COME to one of the most dreaded aspects of true apostolic leadership: fasting. Sadly, over the past centuries, fasting has developed a bad reputation. I believe this has to do with the "carnalization" of the church as far as the aggregate of Christianity is concerned. Many have fallen away from the truth, as well as many others who have not yet fallen completely away, but have certainly ceased preaching and teaching that fasting is one of the most powerful aspects of a true walk with God.

It is interesting to note that the world has picked up on the physical benefits of fasting and is now popularizing it as a method of detoxification, a way to purify the body. It is true that fasting has many physical benefits. Any good nutrition or health book will tell you that. In fact, even the Bible describes fasting's physical benefits. Many accounts, such as Daniel's and that found in Isaiah 58, show us these physical benefits. However, more important than any physical advantage is the impact that fasting makes in the spirit realm.

As leaders, we know this. Our pastors and teachers have taught us this for years. So why do we still struggle with implementing a consistent fasting life? Is it a struggle for the flesh? Absolutely! Do some of us battle physical limitations? Of course!

But these should in no way become excuses for people not to fast. This is what has happened to the aggregate of Christendom. Modern Christianity hardly mentions it anymore, and when it is brought up, it is brushed over to get to a "more important" point in a biblical story. How sad! Something that God designed to literally break the chains of bondage and darkness has been cast to the wayside simply because it is "too hard."

As the Lord's anointed, it is imperative that we implement a consistent and faithful life of fasting for several reasons. Again, if you are reading this or have been invited by your pastor to take part in this study, then you probably understand many of the benefits of fasting. Therefore, just like in the section on prayer, we will cover only those aspects that pertain directly to leadership.

Physical *and* Spiritual Advantage

Yes, it is true that fasting brings physical benefits. As stated earlier, it is a method of detoxification, purging the body of harmful toxins. However, there are many other advantages. For instance, it is proven that fasting helps lower blood pressure and cholesterol, which are two things that definitely need to be at healthy levels when dealing with people![3] It is easy to discover all the health benefits of fasting simply by reading a good nutrition or health book as well as our own apostolic authors, who have written phenomenal resources on fasting. So what does all this have to do with church leadership?

As you continue reading this module, you will notice one of many common themes. If you have not recognized it by now, here it is: as a leader in the church, you are called to be an example to others. It's plain and simple. If you live an unhealthy lifestyle, then chances are many of those you lead will follow suit. Fasting shows a great example of stewardship for the body, which is the temple of the Holy Ghost (1 Corinthians 3:16–17).

However, fasting also helps model the spiritual way for those you lead just as much, if not more, than the physical way. Fasting shows maturity in your walk with God, reverence to His Word, and a relentless system of faith that God will do what He said He would do! Obviously, fasting sets many more positive examples for those you lead, but the point is that all of those things are necessary to build an effective relationship with them because they foster not only trust but faith in you and faith in God through you! Moving on, fasting is just as powerful in the spirit realm as prayer. Let's analyze Isaiah 58:3–12 in the context of leadership.

Fasting's True Identity

First, notice that Isaiah begins describing the faulty focus of Israel's fasting. He notes that Israel complained about how they fasted, and God seemed to turn His ear away. God responds with a sobering truth. He says it is because they are so full of themselves that even in their fast, they feasted on their wickedness, violent contentions, and egos!

How poignant, but how true! Many leaders in the church, even today, have been guilty of this. They fast food and drink, but still harbor bitterness, anger, and pride in themselves. Such a fast does nothing for the spirit. It has become nothing more than just a diet. Just like abstaining from things that feed the flesh to weaken it, we must build the spirit up by purging ourselves of these spiritual inhibitors.

God continues with His sermon by highlighting what fasting has become to them: a mode of self-affliction rather than a strengthening reinforcement. Yes, it is true that fasting weakens the flesh. That is what it is designed to do. However, we are all guilty of focusing and paying too much attention to how much a fast weakens us rather than how much it strengthens us. When Jesus fasted forty days in the wilderness, it weakened His flesh substantially. We know this because the Bible says He became so weak and hungry that the first thing Satan tempted Him with was food. Of course, we know that Jesus defeated him with the true bread of life, the Word of God.

We often marvel at how weak and frail Jesus must have been at that moment, while still being able to find victory over temptation. We wonder and struggle with the fact that we fall in moments of weakness, but Jesus was able to overcome it. While on the surface, this mentality may seem to suggest a high reverence for the deity of Christ, it is actually one reason why we cannot obtain the same victory! With this attitude, we become unable to truly accept and believe verses like Hebrews 4:15–16. This false sense of reverence has actually driven a wedge between us and God rather than driving us closer together.

A better understanding of this account is to realize that although Jesus was at His weakest point physically, He was at His strongest point spiritually. Victory came because the focus was on the spirit instead of the flesh. What darkness could be defeated if we stop giving homage to the flesh during a fast and focused instead on the spirit! God said that a fast shouldn't be for the purpose of afflicting the body, but to bolster the spirit. And that attitude makes all the difference in the world. This is significant for leadership in many ways, including obtaining victory for your own life and ministry. But equally important is the fact that it inspires and motivates others to develop a deeper regimen of fasting, to continue steadfastly and faithfully in it, and even to begin doing it for the first time. John said that there is nothing more satisfying in spiritual leadership than to see those you lead grow and flourish in the Lord (3 John 1:3–4). Speaking from personal experience, he is absolutely right.

As the Lord continues in Isaiah 58:6, He begins to expound on what fasting was designed to do. As He explains fasting's true identity, the Lord shows us the effects of fasting penetrate deep into the spirit realm. The following is what fasting is designed to accomplish:

To Loose the Bands of Wickedness. We have undoubtedly heard it preached before—fasting breaks the chains of bondage. While your fast absolutely accomplishes this for you personally as well as for someone whom you may be fasting, there is another powerful piece of this narrative that is important for leaders. The word "bands" comes from the Hebrew word *chartsubbah*, which simply means pangs or pains. This is especially significant since leaders in the church not only have to battle wickedness itself, but also the ramifications and devastation that wickedness leaves in its wake. Fasting, though, breaks not only the bonds specifically, but also the scars and the marks left on the soul of a human being after that wickedness and sin has had its way. Leaders must be able to help mold and shape a person into the image of Christ, and that starts by utilizing this powerful, God-given discipline to command wickedness to leave and demand its effects to follow suit.

Undo the Heavy Burdens. In the same vein, fasting has a way of untying the heavy burdens that seem to weigh us down. For spiritual leaders, this is significant in several ways, but most importantly, it is a weapon to use in the fight against the barriers that keep people from growing spiritually. We understand that life itself throws many burdens at us. Many people get caught in the rat race of this world just trying to make a living and survive. They have family, a job, and other responsibilities that wear them out! On top of that, they fight to remain faithful to church. Now, many church leaders can relate to these burdens as well, but fasting helps us to shake loose the burdens of this world and put our priorities in order. In fact, the word "undo" means to shake or to be violently agitated. Fasting is so powerful, it can undo the knots of life and help us to focus. When you fast for someone you lead, remember that God is using you to undo the knots and chaos of that old burden in order to foster clarity and focus.

To Let the Oppressed Go Free. We can all agree there is something liberating about a good, solid fast. It helps us know that God has given us power over this old flesh through the Holy Ghost so that we don't have to be a slave to it anymore. It is true that fasting liberates the spiritually enslaved, but digging a little deeper, we find some more poignant information for leaders. The word "oppressed" here means to crush or crack into pieces. This aspect of fasting coincides with the others in that it works to reconfigure and restructure. Or, more accurately, it allows an avenue for God to do the reconfiguring and reconstructing. So not only does fasting loose the bonds and shake the burdens, it also gives God an avenue to come in and piece back together the broken shards of the mind and soul. As leaders, regularly fasting for those you lead gives God an avenue to work with the residue. He makes beauty from ashes, and calls those things that are not as though they are! And as God reweaves the tapestry of someone's character, spiritual empowerment in that individual is received.

Break Every Yoke. Finally, fasting is a complete work. What that means is it leaves no stone unturned. If you are bound by something, it will reveal itself in a fast. Fasting, done right, exposes every bit of darkness and works completely to destroy the bondages of the flesh and the spiritual dominion of the enemy, if we choose to rid ourselves of those things once they come to light. Ironically, the word used for "yoke" here is the same word the King James writers translated as "heavy." The fact that fasting breaks every yoke means there is nothing too heavy, burdensome, enslaving, or demonic that fasting can't create an avenue for God to work through! Fasting is one of the most powerful disciplines and tools God has given His children, but when leaders fast for people they lead, their ministry teams and departments experience significant spiritual growth along with the people who work in them.

The Forgotten Ministry of Fasting. Fasting is so powerful, it exposes the dark corners of our lives to the point that they come out and reveal themselves. Think about it, when we fast food for spiritual reasons and really start to get hungry, we find ourselves getting irritable, cranky, and tired. Nutritionists would explain this as your body's reaction to not receiving the nourishment it needs. Interestingly, they are at least partially correct. However, this is more about the spiritual realm than the physical. We find ourselves acting that way because our flesh is trying to exert itself. The same thing happens during any kind of fast, whether it is food, media, or any other sort of pleasurable activity. However, the actual fast is only half of the battle. Once these idols have manifested themselves through fasting, we still have to release them. That is why the Lord continues to expound upon His idea of what a true fast looks like.

Isaiah 58:7 shows us how to truly rid ourselves of these controlling powers. The Lord says that while on your fast, you should feed the poor and needy, taking that which has controlled you and releasing it as a blessing rather than a curse! Be a family to those who have no family, and open your house and your heart to all those who need comfort and peace. Being a provider for those in need during your separation from and weakening of the flesh is a powerful mode of release and will create a new platform of victory in your life. So many times, we stop a fast, and before long, we find ourselves back in the same spiritual condition we were before we started. However, we exert more power over the flesh when we can freely give away that which we are abstaining from.

The human tendency during a fast is to recluse into a secluded place. You can certainly make a spiritual case for this, as it is important to pray earnestly through the duration of the fast. However, we must not hide ourselves from humanity. We must be ready and willing to minister during a fast, because we show God's face through blessing others while releasing those things that have bound us from getting closer to Him.

When we fast with an understanding and a purpose to effect change in those we lead, then unprecedented spiritual growth can take place as the barriers to personal revival have been loosed, undone, reconfigured, utterly destroyed, and released. The last thing to mention here is we will never reach our full potential to influence unless we implement a fasting life that includes fasting for those we lead.

Isaiah 58:12 gives leaders a powerful *telos* to aspire toward when fasting. It states, "And they that shall be of thee shall build the old waste places: thou shalt raise up the foundations of many generations; and thou shalt be called, The repairer of the breach, The restorer of paths to dwell in." Following God's blueprint for fasting will, without question, exert spiritual authority over your flesh, minister to others, and place you in the spiritual position to successfully lead others to a deeper relationship with God.

To be the "repairer of the breach" is the crux of what spiritual leadership is all about. As leaders in the church, you must possess an unquenchable drive to repair the breaches in the walls of people's lives. Also, note what the Lord said about those you lead. He said they would become builders of "the old waste places." It should be the ultimate goal of every leader to train their people with a conviction that they too will lead someday. The people you lead can one day become people who rebuild the wastelands of people's lives. That is leadership at its depth and heart.

Discussion Questions

1. What physical advantages can fasting provide to your body?

2. How does fasting separate your spiritual intentions from your fleshly desires?

3. How can you see a disparity between God's expectations for fasting and what you may have seen in the church today?

4. In what way does fasting prepare you better to serve others through being the "repairer of the breach?"

CHAPTER 3

Bible Study

THERE IS NO doubt that King David is one of the most esteemed leaders in all of history. Sure, he had his failures, but in the end, he proved to be faithful to God. What was the secret of his success? Was it his talent on the battlefield? Partially. What about the mighty men who followed him? This is another good answer, but not the whole story. You see, in all of David's talents and support, he still had to manage these things and lead people to fulfill an overall vision. Therefore, David's secret to success is none other than his ability to know the will of God and how to lead people to that place.

David was an excellent songwriter, comparatively as good as he was on the battlefield, and in Psalm 119:105, he gives us some insight into the inspiration behind his success. The scripture reads, "Thy word is a lamp unto my feet, and a light unto my path" (Psalm 119:105). What powerful words! David held such high regard for the scriptures, he told God that His Word leads him through the dark places so others can follow him toward His will! That is what leadership is all about. Leaders build a bridge in front of them, taking risks and navigating challenges so those following can find their way across the abyss of life.

David's love for the Word of God is magnified exponentially when you realize that what he had available to him at that time in written form was probably just the Law of Moses. Some would say it is just a rule book, viewing it as more of a nuisance than anything else. But David's heart longed for its eternal words. It is quite shameful that many in the church today see the Bible as just a rule book and a nuisance, when David, having a fraction of what we have today, held it in such high regard that he lived his life by it to the best of his ability.

As leaders, we are called to a higher plane of Bible study. There may be those in the church who are just along for the ride, but let it not be said of the leadership that we are ignorant of the Word of God and how to apply it to our lives. As leaders or potential leaders in the church, you should already know the infallibility and importance of the Word of God. Therefore, this section aims to go deeper and to teach Bible study methods and principles for leaders in the church.

The Difference Maker

Many people get frustrated with the language of the early translations of the Bible, such as the KJV and NKJV. Of course, this led to the innumerable different translations that we now see. However, one must be very careful when selecting a translation of the Bible, as even more confusion can be created. For instance, some versions of the Bible seem to contradict other versions when comparing verse to verse. This also happens when people read verses of scripture out of context.

Context is key in Bible study because it gives the reader a canvas on which to paint a mental picture of the Word into their heart. Without context, we just look at the physical words and neglect all of the spirit involved. Reading scripture in context is the first lesson in Bible study for any church leader. We must be careful not to take the Word out of context. This minimizes our credibility as spiritual leaders, but more importantly, it disrespects the Word of God.

I once listened to a pastor explain to a man why we should not use foul language. There are many verses in the Bible that specifically deal with this subject, such as Matthew 12:34–36, Ephesians 4:29, Colossians 3:8, and many others. Any and all of these verses are sufficient for teaching on the matter. However, this particular pastor answered with Matthew 5:34, which states, "But I say unto you, Swear not at all." Now, on the surface, this seems like a reasonable verse to go to when discussing foul language. However, when you read the context of the scripture, you become enlightened to its true meaning. Jesus was actually talking about swearing to make *oaths*, not swearing as in foul language. The pastor defended his choice of scripture and offered no other scripture on the subject. Consequently, the man, knowing the context of this verse, discredited him and walked out of the church! This sad but true story is just one example of how taking scripture out of context can ruin your witness, ministry, and leadership credibility.

Styles of Context. Reading scripture in context involves many principles that will shed light on an already illuminating book. Three principles, however, most clearly stick out as actual methods for understanding biblical context. First, we need to be attentive to the intertextual context. <u>Intertextual context refers to the overarching theme or the broader meaning</u>. Intertextual context is how the Word flows together to create a coherent thought process. Just as in the example above, we can get ourselves into trouble if we do not have a good grasp of the context in general. Taking scripture out of context is one main impasse affecting "popular" Christianity today and is why so many show contempt for the Word of God.

Leaders do this for all sorts of reasons; they may just be repeating what they have been taught, they may have a skewed understanding of the text themselves, or in some cases, they know they are taking something out of context, but would rather push *their* agenda than God's truth. Sadly, we live in a day where preachers would rather fatten their pocketbook and enlarge hell than speak the truth, nothing wavering. But how many times have we been guilty of sharing some verse or thought of scripture with someone without fully studying it ourselves? Maybe we heard someone else say it before, and it sounded good. Repeating things that we have been taught is not a bad thing. It becomes a problem only when we are guilty of not fully understanding their biblical foundations. This can severely hurt our credibility, especially in a world that places so much of a priority on education and intellect.

<u>Another powerful principle in Bible study is to understand the various social and cultural aspects of scripture</u>. For example, a common social and cultural topic is revealed in John 9:1–2 when

the disciples asked Jesus who had sinned because a man had been born blind. The disciples did not ask whether the blindness was a result of sin, as that was presumed, but wanted to know from whose sin the blindness resulted. In that day, the rabbis taught that if a person suffered from a physical ailment from birth, it must have been because the sick person had sinned before birth or the person's parents or grandparents had committed some sin. The rabbis based their belief on Exodus 34:7, which states, "He does not leave the guilty unpunished; he punishes the children and their children for the sin of the parents to the third and fourth generation" (NIV). However, Jesus assured the disciples that neither parent had sinned, but instead, it occurred so the work of God might be demonstrated in his life (John 9:3).

This analysis would be vital if you were ministering to someone who felt as if the Lord was maliciously punishing him or her for some sin that they have committed. Being able to minister on this level actually takes the oppression and accusation of Satan's attack and turns it into a vehicle for the person to live a victorious life. In other words, instead of thinking that God is punishing them, they realize that is allowing something in their life so His glory can be manifested. It creates a deeper purpose of godliness and victory within them. Therefore, we see how things like social and cultural context of scripture are vital in ministry of any kind.

Finally, it is also important to understand the historical context of scripture. The epistles are one of God's most precious gifts to His people. In them, God, through His ministers, discloses and expounds on many powerful principles of a godly lifestyle.

However, when we take into account the historical context of these epistles, as well as the rest of scripture, it gives us a much more powerful vantage point from which to minister, because we have developed a deeper understanding of the context.

For example, many of Paul's epistles include phrases of victory, faith, and power. Scriptures like Philippians 3:13–14 are powerful verses of scripture that speak of victory and triumph in the name of Jesus. However, when you come to realize that the apostle Paul wrote this very epistle when he was incarcerated for preaching the gospel, you get an even deeper revelation!

Many people fall into the trap of thinking the Word of God is disconnected from today's society. However, people find themselves incarcerated today just like they did in Paul's day, both physical and spiritually. When you couple this with numerous spiritual applications, such as being bound by spiritual forces, then the ministry potential grows exponentially. Suddenly, the Word of God is no longer just some "mystical" book where great words are penned, but with little application to today's issues. No, the Word of God is alive, and it ministers to us the same way it ministered to Paul while he wrote under the influence of the Holy Ghost. When we can minister to someone on that level, we can inspire true hope and motivation deep into their spirit.

Of course, this is not the only example of historical context in the Bible. Think about it; physically, the Bible is a historical book written by historical figures. When you combine this with the fact that its spiritual nature is quick, powerful, and cutting edge, you realize God had a purpose in writing everything the way He wrote it at the time that He wrote it. Therefore, every-thing in the Bible has intertextual, social, cultural, and histori-cal significance that can be applied to today's struggles just as they have been throughout millennia. We invite you to a deeper realm of Bible study. One that will push the boundaries of your conventional thought process to develop a richer understanding of the Word of God, so you can have greater revelation while be-ing able to minister in a more profound way.

Tools for Success

To further address the point of Bible study for church leaders, and in light of these powerful insights, we need to understand that there is a stark difference between just reading the Bible and studying it. Although it is vital for us to read the Bible every day so that it remains fresh on our heart, it is equally important that we study it. Jesus said the Holy Ghost would recall everything we have learned of Him from our memory to our forethought. Well, the simple truth is that unless we study, we cannot learn, and if we cannot learn, then what will the Holy Ghost cause us to recall? The Spirit will recall things for us that we learned, and therefore, if we want deeper revelation, we have to study more deeply. Otherwise, we will be left at the same old level of bibli-cal understanding, when God wants us to dive deeper into its depths. Thankfully, there are many study tools available for the aspiring studious leader. Below is a short list of the possibilities. However, when selecting study tools, one must be careful, in that study tools often contain a lot of opinions and theories that are not necessarily fact. Therefore, pay particular attention when reading commentaries, Bible study material, and the like. For the sake of referencing only those tools that will be most helpful toward accurate and precise biblical literacy, these sources have been withheld from the list. However, do not discard them completely, as they do prove to be valid resources to both provoke and develop thought as well as aid in the revelatory process.

1. **Chronological Bible** – The Chronological Bible contains a rearranged version of the canonical order to reflect the writing of its books as they appeared on the timeline of history. This can give us great historical and sociocultural context, as just knowing when one book was written in relation to another can reveal a deep level of truth.

2. **Archaeological Bible** – The Archaeological Bible contains scientific information throughout its pages. This information often includes valid empirical evidence for much of the biblical text and can be a valid resource in Bible study, giving us deeper context. For instance, one version notes the finding of numerous fossils of different animals on the tops of mountains. Carnivores and their prey seemed to migrate to the same places at one point in history. This no doubt solidifies and helps to prove the account of the flood found in the book of Genesis. Apparently, the animals were looking for higher ground.

3. **Apostolic Study Bible** – Study Bibles are a good resource because they include some explanation of scripture as well as give good historical and scientific background for every book. I have referenced the Apostolic Study Bible here because various one-God apostolic writers have put it together, so we would tend to agree with what is written. This is a very good resource for developing context and chaining scriptures together.

4. **Strong's Concordance** – The bread and butter of Bible study is a good *Strong's Concordance*. The *Strong's Concordance* takes words and phrases that we read in the Bible and shows us the original word in its original language, followed by a definition of that word. This is significant because the translators of the Bible often had a different vocabulary than us (those with a KJV Bible are free to call me Captain Obvious). Therefore, as it was translated into English or any other language, a lot of the meaning was lost. Finding word origins and their true meanings gives us a better understanding of scripture.

5. **Computer programs and apps** – The twenty-first century has given us a massive selection of Bible study computer programs and apps for our electronic devices. Because of the advanced nature of today's smart devices, many programs can do everything on this list and more, making them a very valuable resource for Bible study.

Practice–Practice–Practice

Over the years, I have found that teaching Bible studies helps to solidify biblical knowledge. The more you practice, the better you will be at recalling pertinent information. While the point of Bible studies is not so much to exercise your spiritual brain as it is trying to win and develop souls for the Kingdom, there is a level of respect your students will grant you when you are able to minister by recalling applicable information during a Bible study. This respect is an open door to influence that soul toward change, whether it is unto salvation or a deeper walk with God.

Discussion Questions

1. Judging from scripture, where was the source of King David's leadership ability found?

2. Explain how you can study the Bible using the three modes of context and how it can broaden your understanding of scripture.

3. Name some practical tools that can aid in your study of the Bible.

4. How essential is the Holy Ghost in Bible study?

CHAPTER 4

Spiritual Gifts and Fruit

INDULGE US FOR a moment, and imagine that someone just gave you a very practical gift. We don't mean the type of stuff you get in your Christmas stocking. No, this is a tool you can use to make your life better, your work easier, and your ministry brighter. What would we do with such a gift? Would we neglect its significance and hide it away, never even attempting to explore its worth? Or would we put it to use right away and have confidence that the one that gave us the tool knew we could use the advantage it provides? In the same way, God has granted everyone who has been filled with the Holy Ghost specific and useful gifts that are vital to the healthy operation of the body of Christ (Romans 12:3–8; 1 Corinthians 12–14; Ephesians 4:11–16).

Throughout the history of the early church, as well as that of the modern apostolic movement, there exists another common theme among church leaders. Just as they continued in prayer, fasting, and the Word of God, early church leaders showed their faith in the operation of God by allowing the gifts of the Spirit to work through them. Additionally, they balanced this power with the fruit of the Spirit. The comprehension and utilization of these are vital for successful, and more importantly biblical, church leadership.

As we have said many times before, we designed this study to allow for the facilitator to contribute their own materials and experiences, which are specific to their church, demographic, and will include subtle differences in the way some principles may be taught. The goal for this section is not to teach what these gifts and fruits are, but rather how to apply them in your office, calling, and ministry. The following is an exploration into the principles of spiritual gifts and fruit as they pertain to leaders.

The Gifts

The use of spiritual gifts is vital for church leaders, as they help to fully develop the church, building it up unto spiritual maturity (Ephesians 4:11–13). Leaders can use their gifts within their specific ministries to enhance their leadership ability. In fact, one of the ways that you can tell whether or not you are truly called to a particular office or ministry is to see if your spiritual gifts align with the spiritual demands and duties of the responsibility. For instance, someone who possesses the gift of teaching would potentially be a good fit in Sunday school or another classroom setting in the church. On the other hand, someone who does not possess the gift of administration may not fit into a ministry where a lot of planning and foresight is needed. Of course, this is not the only way to explore your calling, because much prayer, fasting, and counseling with your pastor should be involved as well. This is just a good gauge for you and your pastor to talk about when exploring ministry and leadership in the church.

Although we will not delve into the specifics of each gift, we want to highlight some principles that stand out for leaders. First, notice that there is an actual gift of leadership (Romans 12:8). Although there is a specific gift of leadership, this does not exclude others from leadership in the church. Leadership skills in the church can be learned, developed, and honed through the Holy Ghost and sound training, biblical and otherwise. However, some may seem like natural leaders. This is the spiritual gift of leadership in action, and it is very versatile. Those who possess this gift can combine it with their other gifts to fit in many different positions and offices within the church. Leaders with this gift become especially invaluable in smaller churches, where resources are limited and leaders have to wear many different hats.

Secondly, the use of spiritual gifts within your sphere of influence will foster spiritual and physical growth not only in the church as a whole but also in the individuals you lead by allowing the Holy Ghost to work through you as a conduit. The Lord has gifted you with a specific calling for a specific purpose. We have to remain open at all times for the Lord to use us in a given moment. We are keyed conduits or avenues for God to work through us in specific ways. Some ways do not fit as well as others, and some do not fit at all.

As a child, I remember playing with a toy featuring a table consisting of different shaped holes. I recall periodically getting bored with the norm of matching the shapes so they fit through the holes. It was then that I attempted to force one of the shaped blocks into a hole in which it was not designed to fit. Sometimes I would get stubborn, grab the hammer from my play construction set, and try to pound them through. I was never able to get the square block through the round hole. In fact, I wound up breaking the toy altogether. This is much the same with spiritual gifts. We are keyed in such a way that some spiritual gifts fit more than others, and some do not fit at all. We have to be careful to lend ourselves to the callings and gifts God has given to us and not get bored with the corresponding ministry service they provide. If we try to force a gift without being specifically directed by the Holy Ghost, then we run the risk of breaking ourselves as well as the lives we hold in our hands.

There are twenty total spiritual gifts found in the scripture. These gifts are taken from three main texts found in the epistles to the churches. The following table shows categories of gifts, specific gifts, and where they can be found in scripture.

Category	Gifts	Scripture
Power Gifts	Faith Miracles Healings	1 Corinthians 12
Serving Gifts	Helps/Hospitality Administration Giving Mercy	1 Corinthians 12 Romans 12 1 Peter 4:9-11
Speaking Gifts	Diverse Tongues Interpretation of Tongues Prophecy Teaching Encouragement	1 Corinthians 12 Romans 12
Knowing Gifts	Word of Knowledge Word of Wisdom Discerning of Spirits	1 Corinthians 12
Official Gifts	Apostles Prophets Evangelists Pastor-Teachers Leadership	Romans 12 Ephesians 4

These gifts have been grouped together in categories based on how they relate together in principle. Notice how there is only one category that deals specifically with speaking—only five of the twenty gifts actually involve the spoken word. That's because spiritual leaders, and all saints in general for that matter, need to spend much more time in prayer and thought than they do talking (James 1:19). However, some would rather take the microphone without any meaningful thing to say than minister on the periphery or on the front lines where people who need spiritual guidance are fighting the battles of their lives.

The principle and quality of being slow to speak becomes even more important when you consider again that you hold the lives and souls of those you lead in your hands through the commission of God. Everything you say can be potentially damaging or uplifting. For example, the Lord may give you the Word of wisdom or Word of knowledge about someone or a certain situation. This is the Lord's wisdom and knowledge that He gives for a specific purpose at a specific time (1 Corinthians 12:8–11). Now, as a leader to the particular soul or souls involved, you have power over how you use that knowledge. At that time, the next decision you make will impact their life forever. Some would prefer to divulge that information to their pastor, and rightfully so, depending on the severity of the issue. Still, some others would like to approach that person individually, again taking into account the severity of the issue. Some things should only be handled by your pastor. However, other things should fall to the leader to work through, but not without proper and diligent prayer and fasting.

We should pray diligently for wisdom on how to use our gifts. We should pray that God uses us in the gifts to build His Church (1 Corinthians 12:31). Now, having made the decision through the Holy Ghost to go to that person directly, take caution. It would be best to allow the Word that has been given to you to transition to other gifts, such as encouragement and teaching—that is if they are at your disposal. But the main thing is that you allow God to work through you and do not allow your own carnal biases to get involved. It is situations like this that make the fruit of the Spirit so vital in a leader's ministry.

The Fruit

The fruit of the Spirit found in Galatians 5:22–23 is not just a good Sunday school lesson for children. Actually, your fruit is *the* thing that will identify you. Jesus said that you would know a man by the fruit he bears (Matthew 12:33; Luke 6:44). Therefore, you are known by what is hanging on your branches. What do people think when they see you approaching? Whatever they think, you can be sure it has been influenced to some degree by the fruit, or lack thereof, that you have shown. We will not delve into the specifics of each fruit, but only give you some insight as to what this means for the spiritual leader.

Why is this principle so crucial in spiritual leadership? Because plants reproduce themselves! In case you have not gotten it yet, here it is again in plain English—if you are a bad apple yourself, then you will produce more bad apples! If your tree has a disease, then you will produce more diseased trees. But Jesus said that good trees produce good fruit (Matthew 7:15–20). The fruit that you bear will only be good if you genuinely allow the Holy Ghost to work through you and destroy that carnal nature. The fruit we see here is twofold.

First, it means the fruit of our own personal lives. We are what we do. It doesn't matter if we mean well if our actions show that we do not. Now, it begins with pure intentions, but those pure intentions have to manifest themselves into godly actions in order for any quality fruit to be produced. It is like how a seed produces the actual plant. Your intentions are seeds in the fertile ground of your heart, which can produce fruit in the form of godly actions. Secondly, it refers to the next tree or plant that was reproduced from the original. If your tree produces quality fruit itself, then it is almost certain your offspring will too. This is the crux of spiritual leadership. We have to strive to be our best so that we can minister to others in such a way as to inspire them to be their best.

However, just because we may be quality trees producing quality fruit, that does not mean we are exempt from spiritual trials. In fact, Jesus said those same good trees that produce good fruit will eventually get pruned so they can produce more fruit (John 15:1–6). There are seasons of pruning for every one of God's leaders whom He intends to use in any meaningful way. I have heard my pastor, David Akers, tell me directly while in my own season of pruning, something that will forever burn in my heart. He said, "God will not use you greatly until He can hurt you deeply." This is so true on many different levels, and there are so many examples in scripture from the patriarchs Moses, Abraham, Isaac, and Jacob, to the prophets Isaiah and Jeremiah, to the kings David and Hezekiah, among many others.

It would be easy for you, while in your season of pruning, to become bitter and weary. However, if we know anything personally in spiritual leadership, it is endurance and patience. The pruning season is sure to come for the spiritual leader; it cannot be avoided. However, be encouraged in the fact that your trial is only a season of pruning, and that the Gardener is only trying to make you better and more useful to His work. When this season is over, you will be able to produce more fruit, both in quality and in quantity, as well as minister on a higher plane and deeper level for the glory of God.

This season of pruning is so much better than the alternative. Jesus also said that every tree not bearing good fruit will be cut down and burned (Matthew 7:15–20). We have all heard it preached with the point of being cast into the lake of fire for not producing godly fruit in our lives, and I believe that wholeheartedly. However, I can't help but think there is something more to it. Think about the leadership implications this verse puts on the table.

First, what if Jesus was talking about the kind of people church leaders produce, as well as their own personal fruit. This interpretation would line up with God's leadership expectations. We have to be diligent in our leadership. It is not a game. There are lives and souls at stake, and the Lord will hold us accountable. Don't think that we will be exempt from some form of judgment on the day we stand before Him. Yes, the pastor will accept the brunt of accountability for the souls he influenced. However, other church leaders can expect to hear from God about how they led as well.

Secondly, we assume that fire only means hellfire, and it does mean that. But there is another parallel to spiritual leadership. If we do not produce good fruit in our lives, we can expect nothing less than to get burned, even in this world. Not being a leader with a strong moral compass will most certainly lead to questionable actions that will destroy your ministry. Also, not being peaceful will cause you to get burned by a life of contention and strife. We must allow ourselves to be teachable by the influence of the Holy Ghost and the spiritual leadership placed over us. This will cultivate the ground of the heart and help to ensure the growth of good and precious fruit.

Finally, the key to a fruitful life in the spirit is how well we weed the garden. What we mean by that is how well we crucify our old nature so that the nature of God can flow through us. This is why Paul coupled the list of the fruit in Galatians 5:22–23 with the supporting verses 24–26. If we allow those old weeds to grow, they will certainly choke out all the good fruit. Then we run the risk of being cut down or dying out. Jesus cursed the fig tree that did not have any fruit (Mark 11:13–14). It is easy to look at this example and write it off as something that could not be helped. After all, Mark makes note that it was not the season for figs, so it makes sense, at least on a shallow level, that there were no figs. But Jesus cursed it for a reason. He did it to show His followers the power of God if they would just have faith, but once again, let's look at the implications.

The most powerful implication is found when we recognize Jesus cursed the tree even though it "couldn't help" the fact that it didn't bear any fruit. However, the Lord wanted to show us something, and it pertains directly to the fruit of the Spirit and spiritual leadership. He does nothing without a specific purpose. You see, it was according to the natural or worldly standard that the season for figs had not come yet.

Too many times, spiritual leaders err by allowing their leadership actions, thoughts, and otherwise to be dictated, or at least influenced, by the worldly standard. We have one standard and one standard only: Jesus Christ. We cannot look only to the world's definition of what leadership should look like and expect to bear the fruit God wants us to possess. The world will tell you that temperance means you can look at a woman lustfully, and as long as you don't touch her, it is OK. The world will say joy can only be found in a bottle of alcohol or pills. These notions are appalling! It's time to stop being influenced by the direction of the world's leaders and start following the true Leader. That is why He could look at that fig tree and curse it. It simply was not bearing fruit when Jesus wanted it to regardless of the season it was in.

This is a powerful segue into something the fruit of the Spirit is designed to cultivate—holiness. We would not so much as dare to usurp authority over the spiritual leadership in your life by trying to list specific standards of holiness. Now, we believe wholeheartedly in being holy on the outside, but it is your pastor's responsibility to preach outward standards of holiness as God has led him. We will, however, talk about the source of that outward holiness, no matter the actual shape it may take. That source is the Holy Ghost working in us unto inward holiness. Jesus said that if we would clean the inside of our vessel, then the outside would get washed in the process (Matthew 23:26). Let us not be guilty of putting on a decorative façade to hide the dead man's bones and uncleanness within.

Finally, if we could leave you any last words on the gifts and the fruit of the Spirit, it would be to earnestly strive to display, hone, and utilize them in your personal walk with God as well as in your area of leadership. This means we must have discipline to refuse those sinful things that the flesh desires. Leadership is a powerful life, but it is also a very disciplined life. Paul warned Timothy not to get entangled in the affairs of this world because they would destroy both him and his ministry (2 Timothy 2:1–5). He said that soldiers and athletes do not partake of and get distracted by the things on the periphery. They are dedicated and disciplined so as to not fall out of good favor with the captain. They are focused and temperate so as to not fail in the competition. If we would really truly believe that we are God's champions, would we want those things as much as we do? Pray for temperance and discipline. Pray that God will grant you power to withstand temptation, wisdom to use the gifts He has given, and the personal spirit to display the fruit He commands us to have in every season.

Discussion Questions

1. How do the fruit and gifts impact your leadership ability?

2. What are your spiritual gifts?

3. How have you used your gifts to minister?

4. Explain why it is vital for leaders to display the fruit of the Spirit at all times, even during their challenging seasons.

CHAPTER 5

Empowerment of the Holy Ghost

MANY SCHOLARS AGREE that when the Lord ascended, there were 500 people present to witness the glorious event. Scripture is not clear about how many were actually there, but it is unlikely the Lord lacked an audience, especially given the fact that thousands gathered around Him while He was alive at the first. Logically speaking, how much more so should it have been after His resurrection? Even if it was not the 500 that Paul spoke of in 1 Corinthians 15:6, we can certainly agree that it was probably a lot more than the 120 found in Acts 2. Let's analyze this event and the events surrounding it to illustrate one critical component of apostolic leadership: the empowerment of the Holy Ghost in the leader's life.

If, in fact, as many as 500 saw the Lord's glorious ascension, then it is interesting to note that just ten days later, only 120 were still seeking the promises Jesus gave them on the Mount of Olives. We can speculate quite a bit on why so many fell away so quickly. Many have preached, including myself, that those people simply let the flesh win, or they couldn't handle the persecution. They fell away because they couldn't persevere, for the spirit is willing, but the flesh is weak. However, because scripture is so vague regarding the source of the problem, we can infer some other things that may help to shed some light on this tragic event, or at least help explain how it became so egregious.

For instance, where was the leadership of the apostles when these people were slipping out the back door? Yes, they were praying for the promise. They also spent time trying to fix the broken leadership team that Judas all but destroyed. Now, I am not saying that we should stop, cut short, or skimp on our disciplines (if you think that, then you obviously didn't read the first part of this section). Nor am I advocating for no structure, for Paul told us to do all things decently and in order (1 Corinthians 14:40). However, it is the business of the leader to motivate, inspire, and empower their people to persevere, even when they get weary in well-doing. I believe that the apostles tried to keep people focused. I just can't comprehend how they could have spent three and a half years with the most benevolent person to ever live and not care. Nobody ever reached more than Jesus, and if He taught them anything, it was how to love people. So what went wrong? How could all those people so easily slip away just ten days after seeing Jesus ascend into heaven? Well, simply put, they had not received the Holy Ghost yet!

Jesus said, "But ye shall receive power, after that the Holy Ghost is come upon you: and ye shall be witnesses unto me both in Jerusalem, and in all Judaea, and in Samaria, and unto the uttermost part of the earth" (Acts 1:8). He told them that the source of their leadership empowerment would come from the Holy Ghost. Through the power of the Spirit, they would have the ability to be a witness. What kind of difference does the Holy Ghost make? Well, without it, their leadership ability was nil! Before Jesus was crucified, all they did was argue over which one of them was the greatest and get scared to death during every storm that came their way. Furthermore, to bring it back home, they let hundreds of people fall away! They just didn't have the leadership unction that they needed to have. However, everything changed with the reception and infilling of the Holy Ghost.

Our empowerment and unction give us the ability to be soul winners. Every Christian should strive to win souls, but leaders in the church should make it their specific business. Otherwise, where or to whom are you leading them if not to Christ? I think if each of us would truly examine ourselves, we would agree that we could all do a better job of making soul winning a priority. Evangelism is the church's business. It is the mission, the Great Commission, which Jesus left us with before He ascended into glory! Our talents, gifts, callings, personalities, likes and dislikes, everything about us is centered on this one premise. God did not give us these things to be famous. He didn't give them to us so that we can feel good about ourselves. He didn't even give them to us so that we could follow our own desires and seek after positions and authority. God made each of us uniquely and specifically for the purpose of evangelism.

We were created to testify of Him. We are "fearfully and wonderfully made" with different and unique combinations of gifts, talents, abilities, personalities, and callings (Psalm 139:14). However, none of that is to any avail without the Holy Ghost.

The Holy Ghost is the *active* ingredient that defines the product. When we received the Holy Ghost, it activated our whole unique identity to be a powerful catalyst for apostolic revival.

There are three specific areas where you can put your empowered identity to action: communicating the gospel, communicating your testimony, and living as an example. While both general and leadership communication is such a large topic that it deserves a section all to itself (please see the section titled "Communication" in Module 2), for the purpose of illustrating our empowerment given by the Holy Ghost, it is appropriate to expound on these without delving into too many specifics about communication itself.

However, before we come to grips with how and what we should be communicating, we need to figure some things out. First and foremost, if we analyze our soul-winning endeavors over the course of the last year, what would we see? Now, this illustration is not meant to make anyone feel bad (although I am under severe conviction right now, even as I write). The point is to bring things to light so we can be who God wants us to be, with no hindrances. Jesus said, "Out of the abundance of the heart the mouth speaks" (Matthew 12:34; Luke 6:45). What is in our heart is what comes out. Therefore, it is reasonable to surmise that what is *not* in the heart will *not* come out of your mouth. That is significant, especially in the realm of evangelism.

Maybe we don't witness like we should because we don't believe it like we should. Sure, we believe it enough for ourselves, but maybe not so much when it comes to telling someone else. So the first thing we have to tackle and get under control is our own belief system. If we will come to the place where we truly, madly, and deeply fall in love with Christ and His gospel, to the point where it consumes our hearts, then maybe it will be easier to communicate it in the way we should.

Also, we approach soul winning with either very high or very low expectations. Either it's so low that we don't even try, or it's so high that we get discouraged when someone doesn't receive it or "see" it immediately. Now, we should all have some expectation that God is going to give the increase when we plant and water. That is called faith in the operation of God. However, sometimes, actually most times, it takes a little while for people to accept the truth.

Studies actually show that it takes multiple times for someone to hear an effective communication of the gospel before they will accept it.[4] That doesn't mean it is some magic formula where all we have to do is chant it three times and souls will be won. No, that type of thinking is silly. What this does show is that those who will be saved most likely have to hear it multiple times before accepting it. Therefore, we should go into soul winning with an expectation that God is going to bring revelation, but also understand that plants don't immediately grow upon planting and watering.

Instead of approaching soul winning with a mindset that success means acceptance of the gospel and failure means rejection, we should change our view slightly to reflect an attitude and determination to clearly communicate the gospel. Once the gospel leaves our mouth clearly and with conviction, it is a success, and the Lord is glorified! Yes, do your best to win that soul, but understand that it may take time. Once we gain control of our own belief system, we can begin working on the three areas mentioned above.

Communicating The Gospel

The Holy Ghost gives us a tremendous ability to understand the true gospel of Christ. As explained in the section above, Jesus said the Spirit would bring all things that we have learned back to our remembrance. However, communicating it is a different story, especially when you factor in your specific audience. Now, I believe that God wants us all to minister to everyone, no matter what age, ethnicity, or gender. However, God has called you to that specific leadership ministry for a purpose. We must understand how to clearly communicate the gospel to those we directly lead.

If you are a Sunday school teacher, can you effectively communicate the gospel to children so they can understand and grasp it? How about those who are called to music ministry? Can you write songs, exhort during worship service, and teach your team with a focus on Christ and His gospel? The same goes for a youth pastor or worker, an usher, singles ministry; everyone should have a specific and unique mode and method of communicating the gospel in their specific spheres of influence.

Communicating Your Testimony

What was said about communicating the gospel can also be said of communicating your testimony. This is because your testimony is an extension of the gospel. In other words, it is what God has done for you through the gospel. It is action to go along with your words, demonstration to go along with what some would describe as only foolish rhetoric. When you communicate your testimony in conjunction with and in the context of the gospel, it's like putting a face with a name. It adds credibility to what was spoken.

Many of us, though, are ashamed of some of the more specific points of our testimony. Some have been brought out of addiction to drugs, alcohol, promiscuity, and pornography. Others have been delivered from abusive relationships or being taken advantage of by sexual and sadistic predators. Many others were the predators themselves. These are all things that are very shameful, and we are right to look on our past experiences with at least some sort of disdain. However, the important part is that we have all been delivered, brought out, and bought with a price! That is the power of the gospel (Romans 1:16). We are new creatures; old situations and circumstances are passed away, and all things are new (2 Corinthians 5:17). The key is that we were once victims, once fornicators, once murderers, once drunkards, but God has moved in and delivered us, changing our identity into someone completely different (1 Corinthians 6:9–11).

In the book of Philippians, the apostle Paul taps into something powerful concerning one's past. He says in Philippians 3:14–15 that we should forget those things in the past in the context of condemnation and shortfalls that once separated us from Christ. In other words, there is no condemnation to those who are in Christ (Romans 8:1). Often, leadership falls short of what God would desire of them because they gravitate toward condemnation instead of commendation. Paul could have easily let his past keep him from what God had planned for his ministry. Before his conversion, he actually had people ostracized, interrogated, and killed for even remotely believing in Jesus! He could have buried that testimony and decided to not aspire to anything in God. However, he refused to let that come between him and the calling God had for him. Sure, he was ashamed of what he did. His shame even shows up in his writings; however, it is bridled and harnessed as motivation to aspire to greatness in God rather than as an excuse to stoop to mediocrity!

Ultimately, we can either let our past experiences hinder God's plan, or we can use them as a tool to follow it. Finally, once all these things are put under subjection and understood in the way they need to be understood, we should press forward toward the high calling of God in Christ Jesus. Therefore, we can use those past experiences to foster hope in someone else, whether it is someone you are witnessing to for the first time, someone with whom you have established a relationship, or even someone you are directly responsible for, like those you lead. We have to be careful with sharing details especially to those who are immature or whose character may be in question. However, this does not give us a pass when it comes to sharing our testimony. We need to find a way to effectively communicate our own specific testimony, especially to those we directly lead, because it is one of the most powerful tools of evangelism, inspiration, and motivation.

Finally, a third method of empowerment given by the Holy Ghost is the authority to live as an example. Being God's anointed means being held to a higher standard than others. This privilege is certainly not a license or opportunity to stroke our egos or become wise in our own conceit. Leaders who have become arrogant and self-righteous have always fallen, and fallen hard (1 Corinthians 10:12). Such leaders become self-serving instead of serving others. However, the honor of being an example is bestowed on God's anointed as a physical manifestation of leadership. In other words, people will follow your lead in terms of acting, speaking, or even dressing in a certain way. Shocking, I know, but that is what leaders do, they lead people to some end. Whether it is down the road of righteousness unto God or down the road of self-righteousness, arrogance, and ungodliness, a leader takes his people somewhere. Interestingly enough, a leader will have people following even if he is lost!

All of this may seem elementary, but the point we are trying to make is that leadership is not defined by a position of prestige or recognition from God's people. Leadership is not a game, as you have souls at stake, souls who watch you for guidance and follow your lead! Therefore, we need to be careful to allow the Holy Ghost to work through us in every aspect of our behavior, including what we say, how we act, and how we dress, to name just a few areas in which people spectate (1 Peter 1:15–16). Yes, leaders have the responsibility to model the way for those they lead. So what if a certain standard or matter may not be a heaven or hell issue? Get over trying to live your life as close to the line as possible, because someone who is following you just might cross it!

Paul illustrates this principle in 1 Corinthians 8 when he gives the poignant example of eating meat offered to idols. In this case, Paul says that, in and of itself, eating meat offered to idols is not what condemns someone, it is eating that meat *unto* the idol that defiles them. Those who eat it with an understanding that God is the maker of all and who ask Him to bless it can have a clear conscience. However, the problem lies in the fact that others watch you. They do not know the state of your conscience. Therefore, when they see you eat it, they assume it is OK to eat it *unto* the idol. How does this apply to leadership in the church?

Well, being a book of principle, the Bible gives us deeper meaning. The overarching principle is that even though something may not be "heaven or hell," it is still the leader's responsibility to understand how every action may affect the conscience of someone else. Ultimately, they are responsible for their own actions. However, what are we going to say to God when we stand before Him and He explains to us that someone is in hell partially because of the example we set? The thought of that terrifies me and motivates me to make the right choices because souls are infinitely more important than standards. The spirit of the law trumps the letter of the law because it's founded on principle (2 Corinthians 3:4–8). Words can be twisted, but principles are timeless. Leadership is a serious calling, and if that means living above what is necessary, then I will gladly do it for the gospel's sake.

If there is anything that God's leaders need to take away from this section, it is this: the Holy Ghost is not just some defensive tool God has given us so we can withstand the onslaught of the enemy at the gates. Rather, it is an offensive force of empowerment that can help you lead others to God or to a deeper relationship with Him. Also, this unction from the Holy One gives us the ability to know the mind, will, and plan of God (John 14:26; 1 Corinthians 10–12). Therefore, let us become that empowered pillar of apostolic leadership God has ordained us to be.

This supernatural endowment comes only through prayer and fasting. In Matthew 17:21, Jesus told His disciples they could not cast out demons, among other things, because of their unbelief. It is safe to assume from Jesus's comments that their unbelief came from a lack of prayer and fasting. There is a certain level of confidence that comes from being in tune with and empowered by the Holy Ghost. People may have their fun, mocking and ridiculing us. However, when their family member is sick or another tragedy arises, whom will they look to? When they begin to face the storm of their life, they usually come to the one who is confident in God.

Other Disciplines

There are many, many more principles of spiritual formation that the apostolic leader must develop. While they are foundational to apostolic leadership, one must realize that every aspect of life is fair game to develop spiritually. Therefore, you must give yourself over to the influence of the Holy Ghost. One way we do this is to take heed of and obey our pastors and the spiritual authorities placed over us. Submission to authority is covered in the organizational development section of this study. However, it should be noted that this is a spiritual discipline just as much as, if not more than, a construct toward the health of the organizational edifice. God has placed that spiritual voice over you for a reason. It would be in your best spiritual interest to humble yourself and mind the wisdom and perspective from which they speak.

Another important discipline is tithe paying. Biblically speaking, if you are not paying tithes and offerings, then you are robbing God (Malachi 3:8–12). Organizationally and biblically speaking, if you are not investing into the church, then your heart will not be where it needs to be, especially while in leadership (Matthew 6:19–21, 19:21–22). If we can't trust Him with 10–20 percent of what is already His, then how can we expect Him to trust us with priceless souls? Again, this is not an exhaustive list of disciplines, as there are many, but it will put you on the right track to receive more direction from the Lord on how to develop your ministry and personal walk with Him.

Discussion Questions

1. In what ways does the Holy Ghost empower you to be an effective spiritual leader?

2. How have you used your testimony to support the power of the gospel?

3. Explain how you can better communicate the gospel more effectively.

4. Describe how your own ideologies affect the way you allow the Holy Ghost to empower you.

Recommended for Further Study

Arcovio, John. *The Way of the Eagle*. US: Spirit Led Ministries Publishing, 2011.

Bounds, Edward McKendree. *The Complete Works of E.M. Bounds on Prayer: Experience the Wonders of God through Prayer*. Grand Rapids, MI: Baker Books, 2004.

Bernard, David K. *God's Infallible Word*. Hazlewood, MO: Word Aflame Press, 2011.

Bernard, David K. *Practical Holiness: A Second Look (Series in Pentecostal Theology)*. Hazlewood, MO: Word Aflame Press, 2011.

Bernard, David K. *Spiritual Gifts: A Practical Study with Inspirational Accounts of God's Supernatural Gifts*. Hazlewood, MO: Word Aflame Press, 2010.

Bernard, David K. *Spiritual Leadership in the Twenty-First Century*. Hazlewood, MO: Word Aflame Press, 2010.

Bernard, David K. *Understanding God's Word: An Apostolic Approach to Interpreting the Bible*. Hazlewood, MO: Word Aflame Press, 2010.

Duvall, J. Scott and J. Daniel Hays *Grasping God's word: A Hands-On Approach to Reading, Interpreting, and Applying the Bible*. Grand Rapids, MI: The Zondervan Corporation, 2012.

Haney, Joy. *When Ye Fast*. US: Radiant Life Publications, 1991.

Haney, Joy. *When Ye Pray*. US: Radiant Life Publications, 1992.

Jordan, J. Mark. *Living and Leading in Ministry*. Hazlewood, MO: Word Aflame Press, 2006.

Peterson, Eugene H. *Eat This Book: A Conversation in the Art of Spiritual Reading*. Grand Rapids, MI: William B. Eerdmans Publishing Company, 2006.

Ramsey, Jeff. *Prophetic Prayer: Praying in the Fifth Dimension*. Minden, LA: Repairers of the Breach Ministries, 1998.

Robbins, Vernon K. *Exploring the Texture of Texts: A Guide to Socio-Rhetorical Interpretation*. Harrisburg, PA: Trinity Press International, 1996.

Stoneking, Lee. *The Five-Fold Ministry and Spiritual Insights*. Singapore: MBM Publications, 2003.

Towns, Elmer L. *Fasting for Spiritual Breakthrough: A Guide to Nine Biblical Fasts.* Bloomington, MN: Bethany House Publishers, 2011.

Whitley, Nathan S. (2013). *The Lost Art of Spiritual Disciplines.* Kindle Edition, 2013.

Module 1 Notes

1 Edward McKendree Bounds, *The Complete Works of E.M. Bounds on Prayer: Experience the Wonders of God through Prayer* (Grand Rapids, MI: Baker Books, 2004), 334.
2 Ibid., 142–157.
3 Joy Haney, *When Ye Fast* (US: Radiant Life Publication, 1991), 95–100.
4 Dave Earley and David Wheeler, *Evangelism Is…: How to Share Jesus with Passion and Confidence* (Nashville, TN: B&H Academic Publishing Group, 2010), 1177.

Leadership Competencies

CORD 2

Leadership Competencies

IMAGINE YOURSELF AS the best possible leader? What does that look like to you? Do you have different skills? Are you more patient? Are you a better speaker? Each person has a unique vision of what a great leader looks like. What can you do to bridge the gap from the leader you are today to the one you dream of being? While it is true that some people are naturally born with leadership traits, there are some things we can do to enhance our leadership capabilities. Every leader who hopes to remain effective must always strive to develop. While it would be outside the scope of this study to name all effective leadership styles, traits, or theories, there are several worth noting that Jesus exemplified for Christian leaders who are striving to reach their fullest potential. These include servant and transformational leadership traits. This unit covers each, identifying some prominent characteristics and constructs that can serve as a self-reflection for leadership development.

CHAPTER 6

Servant Leadership

WHEN SURVEYING POPULAR leadership thought and practice, servant leadership is one model that most closely stands out as a good fit for church leadership. Even though this model is first credited to Robert Greenleaf, Jesus provides a great example of this leadership style, which can be traced back to His teachings in Matthew 20 and Mark 10.[1] Although He used other leadership methods at times, Jesus was the epitome of servant leadership, teaching us how to serve one another. He clearly demonstrates that true leadership is founded in love and manifested in service.[2] Jesus unfailingly modeled servanthood and even when He was weary, He never turned His followers away. Jesus said in Mark 9:35, "If any man desire to be first, the same shall be last of all, and servant of all." God's Word is clear—if we want to lead, then we must serve.

Servant leadership is a leadership theory based on traits, qualities, and characteristics founded on the premise that leaders should be servants first.[3] Servant leaders care for everyone and seek to help people grow personally as well as professionally. Modern servant leadership theory in its secular context has no concern for scripture, which is problematic when seeking to implement its principles in the church. However, careful examination of servant leadership theory shows that it directly lines up with scripture whether the world wants to admit it or not.

Christian leadership is distinctive in its motivation of service and love.[4] A great leader is seen as a servant first,[5] for it is the servant leader's ability to love his followers that enables him to truly serve. The source of a servant leader's motivation and main concern is his followers.[6] A Christian leader will desire to see followers grow and will even sacrifice for them, if necessary. He or she will not be concerned with individual status or prestige, but will serve with humility.

What follows is a brief description of certain servant leadership traits and characteristics that are imperative for Apostolic leaders. As you study each of these concepts, we urge you to examine your heart. Are there areas where you are strong? Do you need to work on some areas in order to be a better leader? If honest, most of us will admit that we need some help from the Lord, especially at different times in our life. At the end of this module, you will find an assessment that can be used for self-reflection and to set future goals in order to develop as a leader.

The following servant leadership characteristics are acquired from a variety of leadership theory research and studies, most notably Greenleaf's ten characteristics and Winston and Patterson's seven constructs of servant leadership.[7,8] While many of the constructs overlap, we have developed a model to aid in conceptualization. There are four main categories: love, integrity, discernment, and stewardship. Each category has four or more subcategories. These servant leadership characteristics are all equally important to develop as we follow Christ and lead others to Him. We examine each in the context of scripture to understand how they are relevant to leadership development in the church.

Servant Leadership Model

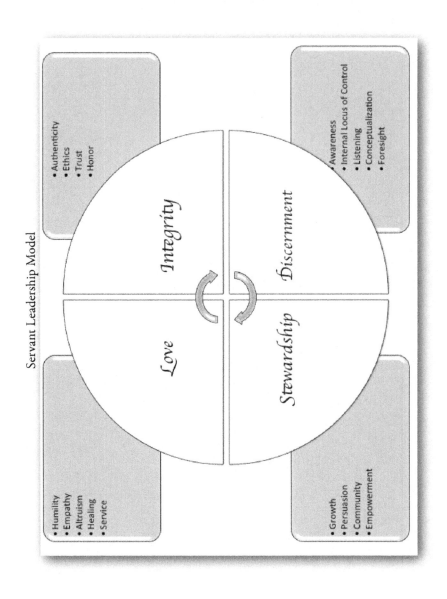

Integrity

- Authenticity
- Ethics
- Trust
- Honor

Discernment

- Awareness
- Internal Locus of Control
- Listening
- Conceptualization
- Foresight

Love

- Humility
- Empathy
- Altruism
- Healing
- Service

Stewardship

- Growth
- Persuasion
- Community
- Empowerment

CHAPTER 7

Love

LOVE IS PERHAPS the most vital trait necessary for any great leader. Jesus stated that it was the greatest commandment in the Law to love the Lord with all your heart, soul, and mind, and to love your neighbor as yourself (Matthew 22:36–40). The scriptures also tell us that love is greater than hope or faith (1 Corinthians 13:13). The servant leader's ability to love is what enables him to truly serve. It is the state of the servant leader's heart, his genuine love that distinguishes him from other leaders. It is Agapao love that is the foundation for the Beatitudes found in Matthew 5.[9] Agapao love empowers a leader to do the right things all the time.[10] It is defined as "preferring to live through Christ."[11] Agapao love is the key ingredient in servant leadership as well as a critical aspect of a person's discipleship. People will know that we are followers of God if we show the love of Christ (John 13:35). This kind of love is always expressed with humility.

Humility

In a society where most leaders are concerned with selfish motives and power, there is a need for leaders who follow after godly principles and morals. However, that raises the question, what does this type of leadership entail? To answer this question, we can look to the scriptures, as the disciples struggled with this same concern. Their ideology was that power and prestige were what made an individual a leader, but Jesus had a different perspective. The disciples wanted to be acclaimed as kings or benefactors of that era, wielding power, receiving honor, titles, and benefits appropriate for their calling of Jesus's sent ones (Luke 22:24–30). In contrast, and for this exact reason, Jesus retorts, "But not so *among* you; on the contrary, he who is greatest among you, let him be as the younger, and he who governs as he who serves" (Luke 22:26 NKJV). However, we know people don't just become younger, thus Jesus does not want the apostles to forsake their duties as leaders, but rather to lead in an exceptional manner that reflects the humble status of youth and servants in the ancient world.[12] Jesus was not teaching His followers that they could not be rulers, but that the manner of benefaction and ruling must be totally transformed.[13] Jesus's own ministry was an example for the disciples (Acts 10:38; Luke 6:35–36; Mark 10:45). The form of leadership appropriate for Jesus's followers is one that is not concerned with the accrual of status or honor, but reflects the humility of servants. He taught us that leadership is not found in rank or position, but in service. Humility is the antidote for pride, which enables one to serve.[14]

People often have a distorted opinion of humility, viewing it as having low self-esteem. However, real humility is a balance of confidence in the leader's God-given abilities and a healthy meekness in attitude, while acknowledging followers for their accomplishments.[15] In the context of the church, humility is power under control, as it provides gentleness and an ability to shun pride. James 4:10 states, "Humble yourselves in the sight of the Lord, and he shall lift you up." The challenge with humility is understanding the difference between a healthy self-image and pride, but the true motives are found in the thoughts and intentions of the heart (Psalm 10:2–4). Humility is also a prerequisite for success in any leadership position in the church (2 Chronicles 7:14). Jesus exemplified what it meant to truly love and serve with humility, so we must model our leadership after Him.

Just as it is vital to serve with humility, it is equally important for Christian leaders to have empathy for others.

Empathy

Empathy describes the ability to place oneself in the shoes of another person and see the world from their perspective, or the ability to partake in another's feelings or ideas.[16, 17] Empathy is important in dealing with people, as it is a powerful means to connect with them. Today, many leaders are often so overwhelmed with responsibilities, they really do not have time to connect with followers. In fact, empathy may even seem to contradict the modern concept of the workplace, which is often viewed as competitive and cutthroat as employees try to reach the top. Organizations often fail because leaders stop focusing on their environment and begin to concentrate on their own agendas.[18] This should not be the case in the church, as the church's success depends on empathetic leaders who are able to adapt, relate to their environment, and build on the strengths of others. As Christian leaders, are we taking time to really connect with followers? Are we only concerned with our own agenda?

Leaders need to not only see and hear the things around them but also be able to relate to the people they serve. For example, burnout is a common problem in churches. Often, people have so many commitments, they tend to work all the time and not make time for themselves or their families. This is especially the case for people who hold secular jobs as well as those within the church, as they have church, family, work, and other obligations to juggle. It is sometimes challenging for leaders who work in full-time ministry to understand where others are coming from, but it is critical to church health that they do. Now, this is not to say that people should start using obligations as an excuse to shun their service to God or get lazy, as it takes the whole body working together. Leaders need to strive for balance and empathize with others to set an example and truly show others how to love and serve Christ. This will help to build relationships between leaders and followers, particularly when people are going through challenging circumstances. In fact, one study conducted by the Center for Creative Leadership surveying more than six thousand leaders from thirty-six countries reveals that empathy is positively related to performance.[19] Another study by Massachusetts General Hospital indicates that empathy plays a role in forging patient–physician relationships, boosting patient satisfaction and aiding in the treatment process.[20] How much more will showing God's love and empathy for others aid in individual and church growth? One may ask, "But how do we empathize with people when we do not understand where they are coming from?" There are several things you can do to become more empathetic.

- Understand how important empathy is to people.
- Be aware of your communication, both verbal and nonverbal.
- Understand that you do not have to agree with someone to understand what they may be feeling and why.
- Try to think about how you would feel in that person's situation and how you would want others to respond; put yourself in their shoes.

Mark 12:31 teaches us to love our neighbor as ourselves, as there is no greater commandment. Additionally, in the Beatitudes, Jesus states, "Blessed are the merciful: for they shall obtain mercy" (Matthew 5:7). The Greek word for mercy is *eleeo*, which means to "have compassion on." The gift of mercy is the ability to have empathy and compassion for people who are suffering and to show that compassion through good deeds.[21] A servant leader will always be empathetic, as empathy aids a servant leader's ability to lead because it helps to build trust with followers.[22] Without the ability to empathize with people, it is impossible to relate to, unselfishly lead, and develop them.

Altruism and Healing

Altruism is the act of unselfishly helping others.[23] A servant leader should not be motivated by personal gain, but by the development of his or her followers. Jesus referred to this principle several times in the gospels and demonstrated it by healing and feeding thousands without seeking anything in return. Moreover, altruism is greatly associated with empathy and healing behaviors.

Healing relates to being made whole in the context of servant leadership.[24] This means the concerns and well-being of others are the servant leader's highest priority, as they often deal with the emotional needs of others. They demonstrate emotional healing by making themselves available to others, standing by them, and providing support for them.[25] Furthermore, Jesus taught us to make ourselves available to heal the hurting, which is particularly evident in the parable of the Good Samaritan (Luke 10:30–37). Many people passed the wounded man without stopping to help. Perhaps they did not have time, were fearful it was a trap, or just did not want to get involved. However, one Samaritan truly showed mercy and love to someone in need whom he did not know. Jesus said that man was his neighbor, and we should go and do likewise (Luke 10:37). When the disciples asked what is the greatest commandment, notice Jesus did not leave it at only the one to "love the Lord thy God with all thy heart, and with all thy soul, and with all thy mind" (Matthew 22:37). He followed with, "And the second is like unto it, Thou shalt love thy neighbour as thyself. On these two commandments hang all the law and the prophets." Yes, sometimes people are needy—really needy—but who else will help show God's love to heal the brokenhearted and lead them to Christ? We should never be too busy to help someone in need. How can you be more altruistic and help heal those in need?

Service

A servant leader's inspiration is to serve followers, to see them grow, and to sacrifice for them when necessary. Service is the main purpose and heart of servant leadership.[26] We see Jesus exemplify service on many occasions in scripture such as when He washed the disciples' feet (John 13:1–17). Through His example, Jesus taught them that leadership is found in service, not in title or position. In other words, Jesus taught that leaders should be servants first (Luke 22:26–27). The difference between a servant-first and leader-first mentality manifests itself in the care taken by the servant to make sure that other people's highest priority needs are being served.[27] In this self-centered world, are we taking the time to serve others? Service comes in many forms, such as being there for someone, working in the church, building relationships with new converts, feeding and helping those in need, and so on. This requires an altruistic and loving nature. Additionally, in order to serve followers best, one must be of utmost integrity and moral character, which leads to our next section of the servant leadership model.

Discussion Questions

1. What is it about love that makes it a central theme in servant leadership?

2. How would you describe the difference between humility and low self-esteem?

3. In what situations do you find it difficult to empathize with others? How can you address this challenge?

4. Describe how you use altruism and healing together as a servant-first leader?

5. How would you incorporate love into your service?

CHAPTER 8

Integrity

Many people equate integrity with being an honest and ethical person. While this is true and a part of integrity, it also encompasses moral uprightness. The very definition of integrity is not only the quality of being honest, but also of being whole, undivided, and having strong moral principles. This is vital for leaders in churches today. We must stand upon the Word of God and not waver in our faith regardless of what others are doing. Proverbs 11:3 states, "The integrity of the upright shall guide them: but the perverseness of transgressors shall destroy them." So we must heed Proverbs 4:25–27 when it says to "Let your eyes look straight ahead; fix your gaze directly before you. Give careful thought to the paths for your feet and be steadfast in all your ways. Do not turn to the right or the left; keep your foot from evil" (NIV). Servant leaders must have integrity, be authentic, ethical, trustworthy, and honorable.

Authentic and Ethical Leadership

Authentic leaders are who they say they are and are true to their word. Authenticity is actually a bundle of other base traits that center on emotional intelligence and integrity and is an inevitable trait that accompanies humility and altruism.[28,29] Authentic leadership is defined as being open, honest, self-aware, confident, optimistic, resilient, and being more concerned about the welfare of others than their own personal welfare.[30] Authenticity helps leaders build a relationship with followers founded upon balance and trust. Both authenticity and integrity are critical aspects of a leader's identity and is vital for church growth. In fact, it is challenging to get anyone to follow if they do not think you are a credible person. A spiritual leader must be seen as authentic in order to gain trust and credibility with those they lead.[31] James 1:22 commands us to practice what we preach by being "doers of the word" and leading by example. Thus, leaders should strive to lead by example, being authentic, in order to get the most out of followers and inspire them toward change.

Some specific leadership actions are critical to the establishment of authentic leadership, particularly in the church. Most notably, authentic leaders must be good stewards of the people God has entrusted in their care as they lead people closer to Him. For Christians, the scripture is the very inspired Word of God, and it sheds light on authenticity and leadership ethics. For example, Jesus condemned the Pharisees because they led Israel astray by their hypocrisy (Matthew 23). Additionally, Paul would emphasize particular ethical leadership traits such as honesty, ethical behavior, and moderation. Thus, a servant leader must be recognized as authentic and ethical in order to gain trust and credibility with followers.

Honor and Trustworthiness

Honor is the quality in a person that describes their integrity. In other words, an honorable person is one who does the right thing even when faced with considerable loss. Today, organizations and their leaders are faced with ethical decisions that put their honor in jeopardy. Integrity concerns the leader's ability to be ethical and honest, which enhances their trustworthiness. However, in today's society, we often hear of leaders telling lies, particularly when trying to support an unethical decision or advance an unethical agenda. Leaders lose the respect and trust of followers when they are dishonest, but honesty begets trust and fosters organizational cohesion and effectiveness.

Furthermore, trust is vital in the leader's attempt to promote a healthy sense of organizational citizenship.[32] Paul explains that leaders should be trustworthy, and places much emphasis on faithfulness (1 Corinthians 4:2). However, problems such as greed and pride often entice leaders to abandon a life of honor, integrity, and trustworthiness. Paul recognized this and urged leaders to be blameless, display good behavior, be honorable, and possess a good reputation (1 Timothy 3:2–10). Thus, it is vital that Christian leaders uphold biblical principles such as "do not lie" (Leviticus 19:11, NIV). Trust and integrity will stem from a leader's candid communication and behavior. Christian leaders with integrity will stimulate assuredness because they can be trusted to do what they say they will do, as they are authentic leaders. Integrity is a measure of whether or not our behavior is pure, as our actions truly speak louder than words (James 2:14–26). Leaders who place an emphasis on honor and integrity will create a trustworthy reputation and culture.

Servant leadership is built on the foundation of trust fostered by integrity and not on hierarchy or position. A servant leader creates an atmosphere of trust where a deeper level of interaction occurs, producing a greater impact.[33] Jesus reiterates this principle when He says, "He that is faithful in that which is least is faithful also in much" (Luke 16:10). Therefore, an effective Christian leader must have integrity and be authentic to gain trust and credibility with followers as well as to be able to discern the needs of those they lead.

Discussion Questions

1. How does integrity affect your leadership ability?

2. How does following an ethical lifestyle produce an authentic leader?

3. Describe the effect that honor and trustworthiness have on a leader's influence.

4. Give an example of a leader who did not have integrity, and describe the consequences.

5. What are some ways to foster trust and authenticity with those you lead?

CHAPTER 9

Discernment

DISCERNMENT HAS TO do with the capability to judge well or in a Christian context, insight in the absence of judgment through obtaining spiritual understanding and direction from God. As godly leaders, our prayer is like the wise King Solomon: "Give your servant therefore an understanding mind to govern your people, that I may discern between good and evil, for who is able to govern this your great people?" (1 Kings 3:9, ESV). We do this so that our love may abound more and more, with all discernment, so that we may approve what is excellent and be pure and blameless for Christ (Philippians 1:9–10). The Holy Spirit will lead and guide us into all truth and give direction in every matter if we seek His face. In order to have proper discernment, servant leaders should be acutely aware of others' perceptions as well as their own in order to effectively lead with vision and foresight to move the church toward growth.

Awareness

Awareness describes a servant leader's capability to be aware and tuned in to their surroundings.[34] Servant leaders are able to see the bigger picture and are not bound by their own perspective.

Awareness enhances leadership effectiveness by awakening the senses to be able to discern more effectively, thus causing better judgment. However, unaware leaders are those who choose to be blind and aloof to adverse issues. Proverbs 6:10–11 states, "Yet a little sleep, a little slumber, a little folding of the hands to sleep: So shall thy poverty come as one that travelleth, and thy want as an armed man." Being passive in every situation does not equate to good leadership. Leaders in the church should be spiritually aware and understand the powers and principalities working in their respective areas of influence. Leaders must stay keenly aware of their environments, having faith that God is in control and taking actions to make unwanted circumstances better.

Internal Locus of Control

Locus of control describes one's belief about control over their future.[35] This is significant in leadership because people tend to view the world through their own perceptions. Leaders with an external locus of control view the future as somewhat automatic or "what will be will be." Therefore, these leaders have little to no interest in motivating people toward change, development, and ultimately growth in God, nor would they be successful at doing so. Leaders with an internal locus of control believe that they control their own fate, at least to a certain extent, and their decisions affect performance. The Christian leader knows that decisions have reactions and consequences, but understands their fate is ultimately in the hands of God (Jeremiah 29:11; 2

[handwritten margin note: Locus: "the effective or perceived location of something abstract"]

96

Corinthians 9:6; Galatians 6:7). This is a vital trait for servant leaders to possess. In particular, locus of control relates to persuasion. Specifically, if a leader desires to be effective at persuading and influencing others, then they must believe they have the power to influence them to change. People can frequently believe a lie the enemy puts in their minds, such as if God wanted our church to grow then He would send a multitude of people. This is not the case; God expects us to do something about it. He wants us to go reach the lost and compel them to come to Him. He wants us to have vision and strive to achieve our dreams.

Conceptualization

Conceptualization refers to a person's capability to be a visionary and provide clear goals and direction.[36] Within the context of servant leadership, conceptualization involves casting a vision that takes into account the personal visions of those we lead.[37] The leader must be able to discern the direction and conceptualize the vision to bring unity toward obtaining the collective goal. Developing this type of vision fosters true commitment to the mission and not just mere compliance.[38] Without a truly shared vision, followers will fade away and lose interest (Proverbs 29:18). This is important in the church because all members need to understand the mission of the church, the Great Commission, is why Christians do what they do. A leader's ability to conceptualize greatly determines whether or not he is able to combine individuals' personal visions of ministry in the overall context of the Great Commission, which is the recipe for successful vision casting.

Foresight

Foresight is a better than average guess about what is going to happen in the future.[39] Past and present events can be used by the servant leader to forecast future happenings.[40] In fact, leaders should be held responsible when they fail to discern and foresee catastrophic events that affect the lives of those they lead. Foresight is a precious commodity. For example, at the close of the Old Testament, we see there was no prophet to predict the coming Greek and Roman invasions. Still today, the capability to be a "watchman on the wall" and to look out into the horizon is necessary in church leadership in order to foresee future events, both physical and spiritual. Additionally, Joseph used his dreams, vision, and foresight to help prepare for the famine that would have wiped out ancient Egypt. Likewise, having foresight will also aid today's leaders in being good stewards of their resources and those they lead.

Discussion Questions

1. In what types of situations have you found discernment to be most effective in leadership?

2. Describe how a lack of awareness can negatively impact your perception.

3. Describe the role that foresight plays in your specific ministry.

4. How does an accurate conceptualization of the church's mission and vision help a leader to motivate and inspire?

5. Explain how a leader's locus of control affects the way they view the need for discernment.

CHAPTER 10

Stewardship

STEWARDSHIP IS A follower-focused form of leadership that empowers followers to make decisions and have control over their work.[41] Additionally, the idea of influencing followers to reach their full potential is developed from the spiritual concept of stewardship. Stewardship involves the leader's desire to take responsibility and help those they lead develop to their fullest potential.[42] It concerns the leader taking responsibility for his followers and ties into accountability. 1 Corinthians 4:1–2 states, "Let a man so account of us, as of the ministers of Christ, and stewards of the mysteries of God. Moreover it is required in stewards, that a man be found faithful" (1 Corinthians 4:1–2). An authentic leader will be a faithful leader. When leaders are faithful to God as well as those they lead, it creates a powerful bond between them, as followers don't second-guess a leader they trust wholeheartedly. The result is a team of fully committed people striving toward the success of the church.

Commitment to the Growth of People

Servant leaders place emphasis on developing people both on a professional and personal level.[43] Servant leaders help those they lead reach their potential and discover their talents. A church whose priority is to develop people understands the power of collaboration and building community (1 Corinthians 3:6). There are several ways to develop people, but the most common are through teaching, leading by example, giving opportunities for experience, and creating a learning environment in which everyone can thrive. It is a leader's responsibility to make sure those they lead are growing in Christ. If not, what can you do to better relate the message and connect with people? We discuss this topic more in the organizational development module. Often, people are hungry for God but just do not know where to begin or where else to go from their current state. Servant leaders will be committed to building relationships with those they lead, helping them grow closer to God in order to discover their unique ministry and fulfill their goals.

Building Community

A primary concern for servant leaders is building community and cultivating an atmosphere where good working relationships can exist.[44] Teams that are unified prove to be more effective.[45] "Behold, how good and how pleasant it is for brethren to dwell together in unity!" (Psalm 133:1). The early church understood the importance of strengthening relationship and fellowship. Acts 2:46 tells us that they continued to meet together every day in the temple, in their homes, and eating together with glad and sincere hearts. There are also many examples of their fellowship and work together to build the Kingdom, such as in Acts 6:1–7, when the disciples empowered others to serve. Thus, a church must be united and empowered in order to grow into a healthy body of good and faithful stewards working together properly, as God designed it (Ephesians 4:16).

Empowerment

Empowerment involves assigning responsibility and delegating authority, providing followers with the resources and encouragement necessary to perform their duties.[46] Exceptional leaders inspire others to action and are capable of empowering them. Servant leaders empower through entrusting those they lead with responsibilities, making them feel significant.[47] Jesus empowered His disciples to continue His ministry by entrusting them with responsibilities (Matthew 28:19; Acts 1:8). For example, Peter was given the keys to the Kingdom and opened the door of salvation to all people (Matthew16:19). Thus, empowerment can therefore be regarded as the act of entrusting power to people and even instructing them on how to use it effectively.

Often, church leaders will need to empower and influence people to develop into what God has called them to be. It is natural to feel insecure or unqualified, particularly when just beginning in a role. Sometimes people feel a call to a certain ministry, and without thought, leaders enthusiastically help get them involved. This is a great way to gain experience and test whether it is a true passion, but what often occurs is individuals are left to sink or swim. This should not be the case, as people need to develop certain skill sets, and it is up to their leader to help them grow. With love and guidance from leadership, people can feel empowered to accomplish the tasks set before them. Empowering others demonstrates good stewardship of those we lead and sets an example of how to influence people toward growth.

Persuasion

Persuasion can be described as a leader's ability to influence someone to change.[48] Persuasion, the opposite of coercion, uses nonjudgmental arguments and effective communication methods. The Bible states death and life are in the power of the tongue; one can either build or tear down with its power (Proverbs 18:21). Building or destroying is largely determined through the motives of the leader. We should be careful what we "call" people to do. It has to be in their heart and in God's timing, no matter what type of ministry we may think they have. Far too often, people are put in positions because they are needed there and not because that is the individual's calling or passion. This can engender discouragement and frustration in the long run if it is only the leaders' desire. There is nothing wrong with allowing people to serve in the church, but it is important to have the right people in the right places according to their gifts, skills, and calling. Thus, the power of persuasion for servant leaders is grounded in the fact that they have the followers' best interests at heart.[49] Personal motives should not be the reason to persuade a follower toward some end. That is manipulation and should never be used, as it destroys and does not build up followers. Even though persuasion can be used for personal gain, servant leaders should only persuade followers toward a goal that builds them up and unites the church. Moreover, servant leaders in the church persuade followers toward a deeper relationship with God. This requires the capability to truly listen, understand followers' needs, and be godly stewards.

Discussion Questions

1. Explain how leaders are actually God's stewards of people.

2. In what ways does a commitment to the growth of people foster church growth?

3. What relationship does building community have with unity in the body of Christ?

4. What methods can you use to empower those you lead?

5. Describe the line between persuasion and coercion.

Final Thoughts on Servant Leadership

In summary, servant leadership is at the crux of Christian leadership. If we are to be great godly leaders, we must learn from the master—Jesus. Everything we do must be done through love with integrity, discernment, and stewardship. The proposed model is not meant to be conclusive of all Christian leadership characteristics, but represents the vital constructs of servant leadership necessary for church leaders. Before church growth and transformation, these traits must be at the heart of every leader. Sure we all have room to grow, but that is why they call it "leadership development." Remember, every leader should always strive to develop in order to be their best for God and have the most impact with those they lead.

We now turn our study toward transformational leadership and its characteristics.

CHAPTER 11

Transformational Leadership

IN ADDITION TO being servants first, Christian leaders must also be transformational in their strategy and approach. The goal of transformational leaders is to impact the lives of followers so they can accomplish more than they had originally intended or thought possible.[50,51] Transformational leaders in the church help raise their followers' concerns from belonging and security to achievement and self-actualization in the Lord by moving them beyond self-interest to care for their organization and the salvation of the world.

Exemplary leaders know they must model the behavior they expect from followers in order to gain the most commitment and achieve goals.[52] They are capable of empowering others to action.[53] We have the greatest transformational leader of all time—Jesus— to model our leadership. He spent time teaching, developing, casting vision, and empowering His disciples. Jesus left a leadership legacy through His disciples that is still impacting our world.

Some of the most prominent transformational characteristics leaders can strive to develop are charisma, being a visionary, and leading change.

Charisma

Charisma is one characteristic of a transformational leader.[54] A charismatic transformational leader is able to motivate followers to go beyond their own interests to work for the good of society.[55] This is a leader who raises followers' levels of ideals, maturity, and concern for the organization and others. A charismatic leader is essentially a very skilled communicator who is able to connect with followers on a deep emotional level in which they are able to articulate a compelling vision.

For example, Steve Jobs was an accomplished speaker who knew how to tell stories and paint a mental picture to involve the audience.[56] He used his passion and charisma to persuade others of the inevitability of his cause and to cast a vision. Think about one of your favorite speakers or preachers, and I am sure you will find the common trait of being great storytellers and communicators.

In order to be effective Christian leaders, we must be able to motivate and inspire followers toward a common goal, effectively communicate, and cast vision.

Visionary

Vision is closely associated with the conceptualization and foresight behaviors of servant leadership, as it requires leaders to provide a clear sense of direction where the organization is headed, taking into account current needs and future goals.[57,58] Effective leaders are able to cast vision and motivate followers to a common purpose. Vision casting requires leaders to consider their own personal vision as well as the visions of the people they lead. This is referred to as a leader's ability to create a shared vision. By seeking God's direction, leaders can develop a shared vision that will lead to success.

Christian leaders must not only strive to meet the needs of followers but also ensure that everyone is working toward the same vision. They cannot be driven by the thirst for prestige, power, or any other selfishness, but rather should be servants first and lead by example. Leading by example will show followers your own commitment to the vision. Proverbs 29:18 tells us, "Where there is no vision, the people perish." Therefore, it is imperative that leaders cast a shared vision to motivate followers past compliance and into engagement.

An effective leader will also give a call to action and then provide action steps in which to accomplish the goals, mission, and vision. Often, we find leaders who are great at casting vision but forget to instruct followers how to reach that vision. It is equally important to know where you are, where you are going, and how you are going to get there. Thus, leaders need to identify a plan to reach the vision. Christian leaders should never get complacent with where they are, but should always strive toward a higher prize, to bring about the transformation that is needed for success (Philippians 3:14).

Leading Change

It is not enough for a leader to just cast a vision for the organization, but the leader must be able to model and lead the way.[59]

However, the goal of the Christian leader should not be so shallow as to only encompass organizational success, but he or she should seek to transform every facet of the organization to align with biblical principles. Of course, leaders should not usurp authority over the pastor, as scripture teaches us they are to lead the flock (Ephesians 4:11; 1 Peter 5:1–7). However, leaders are responsible for being the change agent in their sphere of authority under the direction of their pastor (see pastoral authority section for more information on this topic). For example, the leaders should communicate both in word and example that the organization is not motivated by sinful things such as greed or pride, but founded on humility, servanthood, and other biblical morals and values. This may not be the case in every organization, especially outside the church, thus it is the responsibility of the Christian leader to be the change agent necessary for the transformation.

However, there are certain areas where the church should not implement change, because while we live in this world, we are not of the world (John 15:9). Romans 12:1–2 tells us not to be conformed to this world, but to be transformed by the renewing of our minds that we may prove what is the good, acceptable, and perfect will of God. In these trying times of the twenty-first century, pastors and church leaders can and will be tempted to tweak the message of the Bible in order to fit into a politically correct or culturally accepted box. God's leaders should not be so intimidated by the times that they change the message of God's Word to fit mankind's naturally carnal way of thinking.

For Christianity to remain effective, its leaders must continue to promote it as a distinct worldview. The future of Christianity depends on the ability of its leaders to hold to its foundational beliefs that make it a distinguished worldview, until the Lord comes back for His Church (2 Peter 3:9–13). However, one should not exclude exemplary scholarship and thought concerning leadership principles and skills. At the end of the day, leaders deal with people—not necessarily people as a general "thing," but the challenge to motivate, inspire, and lead them to a positive *telos* in Christ. Thus, we are not referring to change in regard to biblical foundations, but strategies that lead the church to a transformation in Christ. The change will come in time with a consistent and clearly communicated vision through a servant's heart, leading the way to an organization based on biblical principles and submitting to God's direction.

Discussion Questions

1. Think of someone you consider to be a transformational leader; what skills does he or she possess?

2. In what ways can you develop your communication skills to become more inspirational and motivating?

3. Explain how a leader's ability to cast a shared vision relates to motivating those you lead.

4. How does leading change apply to your specific ministry?

Other Leadership Competencies

In addition to servant and transformational leadership traits, there are several other leadership skills that are vital for Christian leaders to possess. These include competencies such as effective communication, temperance, and wisdom, as well as emotional, social, and cultural intelligence. The remaining chapters in this module explore each of these skills in relation to effective church leadership.

CHAPTER 12

Communication

ONE OF THE most vital aspects of effective leadership, and something we all struggle with at times, is communication. In fact, every relationship hinges on effective communication. We are all unique individuals and have our own way of perceiving, interpreting, and communicating things. Yes, there are many similarities in regard to communication, such as the language we speak, but there are also many differences, such as our cultural background, environment, social skills, education, and the list can go on. This makes it particularly challenging to communicate and relate to such diverse people, but it is not impossible, as there are several good communication techniques we can practice to become better communicators and therefore better leaders.

Leadership effectiveness and success depends on one's ability and willingness to learn how to interact and communicate with others.[60] This is because communication is the key tool a leader must use to navigate the various situations and circumstances that arise when leading diverse people through different things. A leader must be able to communicate differently with different followers and in distinctive situations in order to induce a desired response. As Colossians 4:5–6 perfectly states, "Walk in wisdom toward them that are without, redeeming the time. Let your speech be always with grace, seasoned with salt, that ye may know how ye ought to answer every man." This key ability draws certain parallels to the idea of emotional intelligence, or the ability of a leader to empathize, relate, and effectively communicate to followers.[61]

Different situations require different forms of communication. For example, a leader will use certain words and actions when he is casting vision that are markedly different from the words and actions he uses to develop or mentor followers. Any leader would agree that formulating a vision is completely different from actually communicating or casting that vision. Furthermore, a good leader is able to look inside followers and correlate what they see with a special type of leadership communication that fosters motivation and growth in that individual.

For the servant leader, communication begins with listening and being receptive to followers' needs, as a leader cannot effectively serve without listening.[62] Leadership communication skills should be taught with the purpose of training leaders to find "acceptable words" that are "seasoned with salt" and "always with grace," so that they may minister and motivate (Ecclesiastes 12:10; Ephesians 4:29; Colossians 4:6).

For God's anointed, communication starts with listening and being receptive to followers' needs.

Listening
The Bible teaches us that it is better to listen than to speak too quickly. Be slow to speak and quick to hear (James 1:19). Often,

as leaders, we know we have so much to share with followers that we may do more talking than listening. Listening is one of the most important actions of a leader. In fact, great listeners make the best leaders. It is important for leaders to truly listen to what followers have to say and to find a common ground that ties you together. Be open to feedback from your followers and always be willing to learn and grow.

Think Before You Speak

What we say is important, and we cannot take back what is communicated, so it is vital that we think before we speak. Have you ever said something and then thought, "Oh, that didn't come out right," or "Maybe I shouldn't have said that"? To avoid this, be sure to pause before you answer a question or say something, even if your response comes quickly to mind.[63] A little forethought will allow you to customize your answer and make sure your response is appropriate. Philippians 4:8 tells us to think on things that are true, just, honest, pure, lovely, and of good report. If we set our hearts on these things, then it will be rightly communicated, because from the abundance of the heart, the mouth speaks (Luke 6:45).

The Cs of Communication

While the topic of communication is so broad that people write entire books on the subject, here are several tips to help you become a better communicator. Other communication tips are covered throughout this study. We highly recommend further study of communication using several of the great resources already developed, as successful leader–follower relationships hinge on effective communication.

- **Clear:** Your words have to be clear in order for people to understand your meaning.
- **Correct:** Make sure you use the correct words. Mistakes in words and grammar can be damaging. For example, derange and disorganized are sometimes listed as synonyms, but if you say that a disorganized person is deranged, the reaction may not be what you expected!
- **Competent:** Be a competent leader. People have to believe that you know what you are talking about and that you know what you are doing before they will follow your lead. Be open, share what you know and your experiences, and encourage other people to do the same. This will foster trust and confidence in your leadership ability. It is also important to be culturally competent.
- **Culturally Sensitive and Competent:** It is important to be sensitive to other cultures when you communicate, as words can unite or hurt your listeners. Different symbols and communications can have various meanings depending on one's culture. Even our natural languages and behaviors are culturally determined.[64] We see this in the way we learn to speak, what we call things, how we pronounce words, and what language we speak.

Behaviors are even influenced by culture. Understanding a person's cultural background will help you better communicate and be more effective. Thus, it is important to learn as much as possible about their culture to build a relationship and diminish any cultural barriers.

- **Concrete:** Try to make your words as concrete as possible and not abstract. Concrete words are more clear and easier for the listener to remember. For example, "Rascal is a creature," (abstract), or "Rascal is a white Persian cat" (concrete).

- **Color:** This refers to the vividness and emotional intensity of words. Colorful words will paint a picture in the listener's mind. Adding color is an important technique, especially when telling stories or teaching, as it helps keep the listener engaged.

- **Concise:** Make your points quickly and efficiently. As Thomas Jefferson stated, "Never use two words when one will do."

- **Congruent:** Your words and body language should be consistent with what you are meaning to convey. A disgusted face, while trying your mother in law's new dish, and saying it is good will not send the same message.

- **Cast Vision:** Leaders should find a shared vision that will empower followers to work toward the overall vision. It is important to cast vision and inspire followers to work with you toward that vision, but don't just tell them how to do it. Do it with them—model the way. Make sure the message is clear and that people understand how you intend to reach that vision. Set clear and measurable goals, and then celebrate when you reach those goals, because you are that much closer to your vision. We must ensure that we are striving to meet the needs of followers, and that everyone is working toward the same end.

Perhaps one of the most effective strategies when thinking about communication is to ask what kind of traits you want in a leader. How do you want your leader to communicate with you? These are good questions to ask yourself, and then begin doing those things for everyone else. For example, do you want your leader to be honest, competent, and available? Then you should be honest, competent, and available. The Bible teaches us to do unto others as we desire them to do to us (Matthew 7:12). This applies to everyone and everything.

Communication Skills Activities

Following are a few activities the group can use to assess communication effectiveness.

TEAM COMMUNICATION BUILDING

Purpose: The purpose of this activity is to illustrate the importance of clear communication, and to allow the group/individuals to explore their communication style and make improvements as necessary.

Material: Legos (themed Legos work well) or children's building blocks. You will need at least two sets if there is not a picture of the finished model.

Time: About fifteen to twenty minutes (time varies depending on length of discussion and number of times exercise is repeated; allow ten minutes for the construction of the model).

Volunteers: At least four people. You can have duplicate exercises running in parallel if your group is larger, but will need more sets of building blocks.

Instructions: There are four roles:

Person A – director
Person B – material handler
Person C – builder
Person(s) D – observer

Person A (director): Is given the assembled set of blocks or a picture of the finished model (e.g., the cover of the box or picture showing the finished Lego model), and is the only person who can see the object. It is the director's job to give clear instructions to person B, the material handler, so that person C can build an exact replica of the model.

Person B (material handler): Listens to the director's instructions without seeing the blocks (or picture of the final structure), gathers material as needed, and runs to a different part of the room, where person C is sitting. The material handler then passes on the building material and instructions to Person C, the builder. The material handler can make as many trips as required within the time allowed for the exercise.

Person C (builder): Listens to the runner's instructions and builds the object from the set of building blocks. The builder is the only person who can see the object under construction.

Person(s) D (observer(s)): Observes the communication game and takes notes about what works, what doesn't work, and how people behaved under pressure. Person D gives these notes to the group after the exercise.

Listening Activity

Purpose: The purpose of this activity is to illustrate the importance of listening and clear communication. This is a fantastic activity to focus learning on barriers to communication and assumptions we make about communication.

Material: A sheet of paper with shapes and (geometrical) patterns or a picture.

Time: About ten minutes for activity and ten minutes for debriefing.

Instructions:

- Break class into groups of five (or whatever number works well for your class size).
- For each group, ask them to select a leader from among themselves. Give a sheet of paper with the geometrical pattern to the leader. Give a blank sheet of paper to each of the other group members.
- Take the leaders of all the groups aside and instruct the leaders that they have to sit with their backs to their group in such a way that the group can neither see the paper in their hands nor the leaders' expressions. Each leader must explain the picture/pattern on their paper to their group in such a way that they should be able to draw it on their papers. The leader is not allowed to use their hands to gesture.

- Instruct the group members that they have to reproduce whatever their leader tells them to draw.
- Tell them that they have ten minutes for the activity and to start the activity. Observe the leader and the group members and their interactions.
- Stop the activity at the end of ten minutes and debrief.

ALTERNATIVE LISTENING ACTIVITY FOR SMALL GROUPS

Purpose: The purpose of this activity is to illustrate the importance of listening and clear communication. This is a fantastic activity to focus learning on barriers to communication, assumptions we make about communication, and developing empathy.

Material: Children's large block set (at least ten blocks).

Time: About five minutes for each activity and ten minutes for debriefing.

Instructions: There are two roles: the builder and the director. The facilitator will pick the type of structure to build, such as a house, tower, castle, car, etc., and tell it to only the director.

Director: The director will instruct the builder on how to build the structure. The director faces away from the builder while doing so.

Builder: The builder is blindfolded and listens to the director's instructions, doing his or her best to build the structure (Note: large blocks are easier for feeling the shapes).

Switch roles and see what it is like to be in the other person's shoes.

CHAPTER 13

Intellectual Competencies

JUST AS IT is important to effectively communicate, apostolic leaders should also be aware of their own actions as well as possess an understanding of others' social and cultural customs. Leaders use intellectual skills to successfully relate to those they lead. This requires temperance, wisdom, emotional, social, and cultural intelligence.

Temperance

Temperance, or self-control, is vital for Christian leaders, especially when dealing with ethical decisions. Paul lists temperance, along with many other vital virtues, as a fruit of the Spirit that all Christians should possess (Galatians 5:22–24). Many people relate temperance to abstaining from certain vices or other temptations such as alcohol, caffeine, or chocolate. However, temperance also includes the ability to be in control of one's actions and to not be driven by spontaneity, but to be able to accept and live within one's limits.[65]

People in leadership will always find themselves in situations where an ethical decision must be made. Sometimes, this decision could result in unfavorable circumstances. It is temperance that will keep the Christian leader from taking the easy way out by fudging the numbers or committing any other immoral action. The scriptures teach us "to say 'No' to ungodliness and worldly passions, and to live self-controlled, upright and godly lives" (Titus 2:11–12, NIV).

The lack of temperance also directly relates to having selfish motives and intentions, which many business professionals are tempted with daily. For example, making it to the top of the corporate ladder at another's expense. We even regretfully see this in the church at times.

This is why it is imperative that we remain humble in all of our actions and lead with wisdom.

Wisdom

Now more than ever, the world is in dire need of wise Christian leaders who will seek to change the world with the mind of Christ and not their own. Jesus said it best when He stated, "I am sending you out like sheep among wolves. Therefore be as shrewd as snakes and as innocent as doves" (Matthew 10:16, NIV). We live in a dog-eat-dog world, and that mentality is especially alive and well in the corporate realm. Christian leaders should seek to display and practice wisdom through the mind of Christ so that we may be "as shrewd as serpents and as innocent as doves."

There is an age-old myth that some people are born to be leaders, while others just do not possess the skills. However, research has shown that leadership traits can be both learned and honed. What this means for Christian leaders is that we can pray for God to teach us wisdom and help us make ethical decisions. James 1:5 states, "If any of you lacks wisdom, you should ask God, who gives generously to all without finding fault, and it will be given to you" (NIV). Without wisdom, Christian leaders will not be able to look at moral and ethical situations objectively, which is necessary to be just when making decisions based on scripture. Wisdom will also help to facilitate temperance when situations get heated or tense and the potential to lose control and make impulsive decisions escalates.

This is where other vital competencies, such as emotional, social, and cultural intelligence, will serve a leader well in this diverse society.

Emotional Intelligence

Emotional intelligence (EI) has become a trendy topic in recent years, as it is a key component of effective leadership. In fact, 80–90 percent of the competencies that distinguish star leaders are based on emotional intelligence.[66] EI is the capability to effectively recognize and manage our own as well as others' emotions. There are five components of emotional intelligence:

- *Self-Awareness* – The ability to recognize and understand your emotions, drives, and moods as well as how they affect others.

- *Self-Regulation* – The ability to redirect and control disruptive moods and impulses; the tendency to check decisions or to think before acting.
- *Internal Motivation* – A tendency to pursue goals with persistence and energy; a desire to work for reasons that go beyond status or money.
- *Empathy* – The capability to understand the emotional makeup of others; skills in considering others according to their emotional reactions.
- *Social Skills* – An ability to build rapport and find common ground; expertise in building networks and managing relationships.

For many people, emotional intelligence is more important than their intellectual intelligence in regard to their careers and lives, as one's success depends on the ability to read people and respond appropriately.[67] How we interact with and respond to people will either build up or destroy leader–follower relationships. Emotional intelligence is critical for a servant leader because it can help to accurately identify, diagnose, and suppress personal feelings that may impede the serving process. Scripture teaches us to examine and know ourselves (2 Corinthians 13:5).

Social awareness is the measure of the ability to relate to others and is a vital element of emotional intelligence. A servant leader must be able to relate and be sensitive to people to effectively serve their needs. The good news is that EI can be learned. EI naturally develops with age; as one grows older, they mature and develop through life experiences.

One of the first steps in developing your EI involves self-awareness. A high level of self-awareness is vital in order for a leader to not be driven by emotions.[68] From altruism and humility come an increased capacity for authenticity and self-awareness. Therefore, self-awareness is paramount in Christian leadership because of the need to be sensitive to the emotions and issues of others and not be driven by our own.

You can find out what your emotional quotient (EQ) is by taking an assessment. There are also trainings in emotional competencies that include how to empower others and be inspired, become a better listener, and become a more effective leader. Leaders can partner with a coach or another leader within the organization to work on strengthening skills such as teamwork, communication, or empathy.

Additionally, you can focus on developing certain things to strengthen your EI, such as: self-awareness through realistic expectations of yourself, controlling impulses, reading and interpreting social cues, identifying and anticipating consequences and alternative actions, understanding the behavioral norms and perspectives of others, setting goals, helping others, and having a positive attitude toward life.[69] You can also develop your communication skills by ensuring you are making clear requests, listening to others, responding appropriately to criticism, and resisting negative influences.[70] While there are many ways to develop your EI, the key is to understand that it can be developed and then find the method(s) that works best for you.

Another competency closely related to EI that plays a vital role in leadership is social intelligence.

Social Intelligence

All effective leadership is based on good leader–follower relationships. In fact, the best leaders and coaches have a higher degree of emotional and social intelligence.[71] Therefore, it is imperative to have the necessary social skills to be an effective leader. No, this does not mean that one must be a social butterfly. It just means a leader must understand and know how to relate to and influence each of his or her followers. The Bible is full of scriptures that provide guidance on how to treat others, such as be kind, treat them with respect (Ephesians 6:5–9), show love (Mark 12:30–31), as well as being just and fair (Colossians 4:1), which will enhance leader–follower relationships.

Overlapping with emotional intelligence, social intelligence works on the level of interaction. Social intelligence (SI) is our "people skills" or ability to get along with others and get them to cooperate with you.[72] There are also several central elements of SI, including knowledge of social roles, communication and effective listening skills, capability to understand others, being comfortable with all types of people (i.e. role-playing and social self-efficacy), and authenticity and concern with what impression you are making on others.[73] In addition, SI is commonly referred to as common sense, street smarts, or tact. Socially intelligent leaders describe people who show empathy, a commitment to developing others, inspiration, attunement to the thinking and emotions of others, and a commitment to building and supporting teams.[74] All of these traits are crucial for effective leadership.

The good news is SI can also be developed. In fact, it is mostly a learned behavior, and is one of the most powerful tools at your disposal for strengthening your team and your leadership.[75] A leader must be aware of their effect within social contexts if they wish to develop. SI develops from success and failure in social settings and from experiences with people. Consequently, the best method of developing SI is through experience and being placed in various social situations. A leader seeking to increase SI should pay more attention to the social world and study social situations as well as their own behavior by learning from successes and failures.

It is also vital that leaders develop their communication skills to ensure they are effectively relating, perceiving, and being perceived. This is where understanding one's culture can prove to be beneficial, especially for multicultural leaders.

Cultural Intelligence

It is vital for leaders to have cultural competencies in today's global society. Cultural intelligence (CQ) refers to the capability to develop empathy, understanding, and the ability to work with people from other nationalities.[76] One's cultural intelligence provides insight about individual capabilities to engage in cross-cultural interactions, perform in culturally diverse work groups, and cope with multicultural situations.[77] Although cultural intelligence is related to emotional intelligence, it goes a step further.[78] Whereas leaders with high emotional intelligence can pick up on the needs, desires, and emotions of others, those with high cultural intelligence are attuned to the beliefs, attitudes, values, body language, and communication of people from different cultures. They use this knowledge to be able to better interact and lead them. People with high cultural intelligence are not experts in every culture; rather, they use intelligence, empathy, and observation to read situations and people in order to make informed decisions. Leaders will also use cultural intelligence to monitor their own actions instead of relying on stereotypes or making quick judgments; they observe what is happening and adapt their own behavior appropriately. The ability to understand and adapt behavior according to one's culture allows the leader to have a more effective relationship with others.

Like emotional and social intelligence, cultural intelligence can be developed. Developing CQ is essential for effective leadership. However, it is wise to understand that you cannot possibly know everything about a culture, so leaders will need to continually develop their CQ. There are numerous methods of improving CQ, such as training, coaching, personal skill development, and the like. For example, diversity, culture, and cultural intelligence training are all programs that can help foster organizational diversity and improve cross-cultural relations. One of the best methods of improving CQ is through personalized coaching and training based on CQ assessments.[79] Enhancing CQ will give a leader a greater advantage in collaborating with people from various cultural backgrounds. It will also help leaders feel more comfortable in cross-cultural situations.

Paul – A Biblical Leadership Example of EI, SI, and CQ

Paul was a successful biblical leader who exemplified emotional, social, and cultural intelligence. He knew the importance of understanding social context, being able to empathize, and how culture affects people's perspectives. Paul stated, "I have become all things to all people so that by all possible means I might save some" (1 Corinthians 9:22, NIV). Paul made it a purpose to transform the way he thought and to understand other's perspectives so that he could be a partner with them for the gospel's sake.

Several times in the texts, Paul states that he "became." The Greek word for became is *ginomai*, which means "to transition from one state of being to another." Therefore, Paul became like them in thought so that he could win, influence, and transform their ideas. For example, Paul acclimated himself with certain beliefs and laws, he abstained from certain foods and ate meats that were considered unlawful, all to save some (Acts 17; Romans 14:21; 1 Corinthians 8:13). This is why he could state to the Jew, the Gentile, and the weak that he became like them (1 Corinthians 9:20–23).

In order for Paul to be able to relate to and "become all things to all men," he had to be culturally, socially, and emotionally intelligent in order to transform the mindset of his audience. He did all of this within the boundaries of scripture and did not perform, condone, or teach any sinful things. Instead, Paul used these competencies throughout his ministry to propagate the gospel and develop the church.

Discussion Questions

1. What makes the quality of temperance so vital for a leader?

2. Give an example in your ministry where using wisdom was paramount for obtaining a positive outcome in a situation.

3. What can you do to develop your emotional, social, and cultural intelligence?

4. How did Jesus use emotional, social, or cultural intelligence in His ministry?

Strategies for Self-Development

While this is not intended to be a comprehensive list of leadership styles or characteristics, these are some of the most vital traits for Christian leaders. People have their own goals and areas they want or need to focus on for growth and development. Leadership development is a lifelong process of learning. Thus, it is important to frequently assess your current state and develop strategies to get to where you hope to be in the future. Assessments and coaching are two great aids for a leader's development.

Assessments. Assessments can play an important role in generating self-awareness by bringing to light new information, ways of thinking, and ways of behaving the individual may not have seen before, or affirming what the leader may already allege to know.[80] Assessments in general can provide information on selected aspects of the leader's skills, performance, styles, preferences, or behaviors.[81]

There are several types of assessments, such as self-assessments, 360 feedback assessments, and grounded assessments (i.e., based on observations). Likewise, there are several benefits to using assessments, including to increase self-awareness, for personal and career development, to improve productivity, and to solve issues.[82] While there are numerous types of and benefits to each assessment, the key is finding the most relevant assessment.

Assessments are commonly used in the coaching profession, as coaching is about helping clients achieve goals. This process involves both self-awareness and self-efficacy. This is particularly evident in leadership coaching, as most of the focus is centered on leadership development. Many professionals say a good development formula is: "assessments + coaching = development."[83]

Coaching. Leader development is one of the most important aspects of organizational effectiveness and growth. Churches that place a high priority on leader development are concerned with their well-being and future. Coaching is a tool that helps individuals and organizations get from where they are currently to where they would like to be in the future.[84] In other words, it helps them realize and obtain future goals.

Coaching does not involve giving expert advice or solutions, like consulting, but instead involves listening, asking insightful questions, and guiding a person to make his or her own decisions and take actions to reach their goals.[85] Coaching allows a leader to receive crucial feedback on current key behavioral strengths and weaknesses in order to effect change that results in a positive perception by others within the organization.[86] Additionally, coaching brings many benefits to clients, including greater interpersonal effectiveness, increased confidence, enhanced decision-making skill, and new perspectives on personal challenges.[87] Thus, finding a coach is a great strategy for leader development. For more information on coaching, please see Appendix A.

In addition to self-awareness and development, a leader must also focus on developing the organization, which brings us to our third cord: organizational development.

Activity

Complete the following assessments found in Appendices B, C, and D: Servant Leadership, Transformational, and Communication.

Module 2 Notes

1 Robert K. Greenleaf, *Servant Leadership: A Journey into the Nature of Legitimate Power and Greatness* (Mahwah, NJ: Paulist Press, 2002).

2 Ted W. Engstrom, *The Making of a Christian Leader: How to Develop Management and Human Relations Skills* (Grand Rapids, MI: The Zondervan Corporation, 1976), 37.

3 Greenleaf, *Servant Leadership*, 27–28.

4 Engstrom, *The Making of a Christian Leader*, 37.

5 Greenleaf, *Servant Leadership*, 27–28.

6 John J. Sullivan, *Servant First! Leadership for the New Millennium* (Maitland, FL: Xulon Press, 2004), 123–142.

7 Greenleaf, *Servant Leadership*.

8 Bruce Winston and Kathleen Patterson, "An Integrative Definition of Leadership," *International Journal of Leadership Studies*, 1, no. 2 (2006): 6–66.

9 Winston and Patterson, "An Integrative Definition of Leadership," 6–66.

10 Ibid.

11 "Agapao," *Strong's Greek Concordance Online* on Biblesuite.com, 2013, http://concordances.org/greek/25.htm.

12 Peter Nelson, *Leadership and Discipleship: A Study of Luke 22:24–30 (Society of Biblical Literature Dissertation Series)* (Atlanta: The Society of Biblical Literature, 1994).

13 Don B. Garlington, "Who is the Greatest," *Journal of the Evangelical Theological Society, JETS* 53, no.2, (June 2010): 305–307. http://0-ehis.ebscohost.com.library.regent.edu/eds/detail?vid=3&sid=f9427620-1a1f-4f35-97b5-4b5f3cc7c4a3%40sessionmgr4&hid=3&bdata=JnNpdGU9ZWRzLWxpdmU%3d.

14 Kathleen Patterson, "Humility: The Queen of Virtues," YouTube video, 19:17, from Virtual Conference on Moral Leadership: Humility and Organizational Leadership, posted by Regent University's School of Business & Leadership, December 8, 2011, http://www.youtube.com/watch?v=lAvOuhH8pCk.

15 Winston and Patterson, "An Integrative Definition of Leadership," 6–66.

16 Peter G. Northouse, *Leadership: Theory and Practice*, 6th ed. (Thousand Oaks, CA: SAGE Publications, Inc., 2013), 219–232.

17 Larry C. Spears and Michele Lawrence, *Practicing Servant-Leadership: Succeeding Through Trust, Bravery, and Forgiveness* (San Francisco: Jossey-Bass, 2004), 135–137.

18 Jayson Boyers, "Why Empathy Is The Force That Moves Business Forward," *Forbes* (blog), May 20, 2013, http://www.forbes.com/sites/ashoka/2013/05/30/why-empathy-is-the-force-that-moves-business-forward/.

19 David F. Swink, "I Don't Feel Your Pain: Overcoming Roadblocks to Empathy," *Psychology Today* (blog), March 7, 2013, https://www.psychologytoday.com/blog/threat-management/201303/i-dont-feel-your-pain-overcoming-roadblocks-empathy.

20 Ibid.

21 Dorena DellaVecchio, PhD, and Bruce E. Winston, PhD, "A Seven-Scale Instrument to Measure the Romans 12 Motivational Gifts and a Proposition that the Romans 12 Gift Profiles Might Apply to Person–Job Fit Analysis" (working paper, School of Leadership Studies, Regent University, Virginia Beach, VA, October 2004). http://www.regent.edu/acad/global/publications/working/DellaVecchio-Winston%20Romans%2012%20gift%20test%20and%20profiles%20manuscriptdv.pdf.

22 Greenleaf, *Servant Leadership*, 33–35.

23 Winston and Patterson, "An Integrative Definition of Leadership," 6–66.

24 Northouse, *Leadership: Theory and Practice*, 219–232.

25 Ibid., 227.

26 Winston and Patterson, "An Integrative Definition of Leadership," 6–66.

27 Greenleaf, *Servant Leadership*, 27.

28 Andrew J. Dubrin, *Fundamentals of Organizational Behavior*, 4th ed. (Mason, OH: Cengage Learning, 2007), 235.

29 Randy Poon, "A Model for Servant Leadership, Self-Efficacy and Mentorship" (Servant Leadership Research Roundtable, Regent University School of Leadership, Virginia Beach, VA, August, 2006), https://regent.blackboard.com.

30 Dubrin, *Fundamentals of Organizational Behavior*, 235.

31 J. Oswald Sanders, *Spiritual Leadership: Principles of Excellence for Every Believer (Commitment to Spiritual Growth)* (Chicago: Moody Publishers, 2007).

32 Robert N. Lussier and Christopher F. Achua, *Leadership: Theory, Application & Skill Development*, 5th ed. (Mason, OH: Thomson South-Western, 2007), 39.

33 Winston and Patterson, "An Integrative Definition of Leadership," 6–66.

34 Northouse, *Leadership: Theory and Practice*, 222.

35 Lussier and Achua, *Leadership: Theory, Application & Skill Development*, 262.

36 Northouse, *Leadership: Theory and Practice*, 222.

37 Winston and Patterson, "An Integrative Definition of Leadership," 6–66.

38 Peter M. Senge, *The Fifth Discipline: The Art & Practice of the Learning Organization* (New York: Doubleday, 2006), 207–209.

39 Greenleaf, *Servant Leadership*, 38.

40 Northouse, *Leadership: Theory and Practice*, 222.

41 Lussier and Achua, *Leadership: Theory, Application & Skill Development*, 357.

42 Northouse, *Leadership: Theory and Practice*, 222.

43 Ibid., 222–223.

44 Northouse, *Leadership: Theory and Practice*, 222–223.

45 J. Richard Hackman, *Leading Teams: Setting the Stage for Great Performances* (Boston: Harvard Business School Press, 2002), 28–35.

46 Sullivan, *Servant First! Leadership for the New Millennium*, 107–142.

47 Winston and Patterson, "An Integrative Definition of Leadership," 6–66.

48 Northouse, *Leadership: Theory and Practice*, 222.

49 Greenleaf, *Servant Leadership*, 42–44.

50 Bernard M. Bass, *The Bass Handbook of Leadership: Theory, Research, and Managerial Applications*, 4th ed. (New York: Free Press, 2008), 618–648.

51 James MacGregor Burns, *Leadership* (London: Harper Torchbooks, 1978).

52 James Kouzes and Barry Posner, *The Leadership Challenge: How to Make Extraordinary Things Happen in Organizations*, (San Francisco: Jossey-Bass, 2012), 71–97.

53 Northouse, *Leadership: Theory and Practice*, 185–211.

54 Ibid., 187–189.

55 Bass, *The Bass Handbook of Leadership*, 618–620.

56 Ronald E. Riggio, PhD, "What Is Charisma and Charismatic Leadership?" *Psychology Today* (blog), October 7, 2012, http://www.psychologytoday.com/blog/cutting-edge-leadership/201210/what-is-charisma-and-charismatic-leadership.

57 Greenleaf, *Servant Leadership*, 79–82.

58 Northouse, *Leadership: Theory and Practice,* 197–205.

59 Kouzes and Posner, *The Leadership Challenge,* 96.

60 Michael Z. Hackman and Craig E. Johnson, *Leadership: A Communication Perspective,* 5th ed. (Long Grove, IL: Waveland Press, 2009), 11.

61 Lussier and Achua, *Leadership: Theory, Application & Skill Development,* 189–197.

62 Spears and Lawrence, *Practicing Servant-Leadership,* 145–137.

63 Dianna Booher, *Speak With Confidence: Powerful Presentations That Inform, Inspire, and Persuade* (New York: McGraw-Hill, 2003), 145–166.

64 Frank E.X. Dance, "A Speech Theory of Human Communication: Implications and Applications," *Journal Of Applied Communication Research* 10, no.1 (February, 1982): 1–8.

65 Kyle D. Fedler, *Exploring Christian Ethics: Biblical Foundations for Morality* (Louisville, KY: Westminster John Knox Press, 2006), 44.

66 Daniel Goleman, "What It Takes to Achieve Managerial Success," *TD: Talent Development* 68, no. 11 (November 8, 2014), 48.

67 Michael Akers and Grover Porter, "What is Emotional Intelligence (EQ)?" *PsychCentral,* last modified October 6, 2015, http://psychcentral.com/lib/what-is-emotional-intelligence-eq/.

68 Poon, "A Model for Servant Leadership, Self-Efficacy and Mentorship," 6.

69 Ibid.

70 Hackman and Johnson, *Leadership: A Communication Perspective,* 166–195.

71 Gary R. Collins, PhD, *Christian Coaching: Helping Others Turn Potential Into Reality,* 2nd ed.(Colorado Springs, CO: NavPress, 2009).

72 Karl Albrecht, "Social Intelligence Theory," 2004, https://www.karlalbrecht.com/siprofile/siprofiletheory.htm.

73 Riggio, "What Is Charisma and Charismatic Leadership?" 2012.

74 Collins, *Christian Coaching,* 896–904.

75 Riggio, "What Is Charisma and Charismatic Leadership?" 2012.

76 Edgar H. Schein, *Organizational Culture and Leadership,* 4th ed. (San Francisco: Jossey-Bass, 2010), 387–389.

77 Cultural Intelligence Center, "What is CQ?" 2015, http://www.culturalq.com/tmpl/research/about.php.

78 Mind Tools, "Cultural Intelligence: Working Successfully With Diverse Groups," *Mindtools,* 2015, http://www.mindtools.com/pages/article/cultural-intelligence.htm.

79 Cultural Intelligence Center, "What is CQ?" 2015.

80 Mary Beth O'Neill, *Executive Coaching with Backbone and Heart: A Systems Approach to Engaging Leaders with Their Challenges,* 2nd ed. (San Francisco: Jossey-Bass, 2007).

81 Sue E. McLeod, "Assessments for Insight, Learning, and Choice in Coaching," in *On Becoming a Leadership Coach: A Holistic Approach to Coaching Excellence,* eds. Christine Wahl, Clarice Scriber, and Beth Bloomfield (New York: Palgrave Macmillan, 2013), 207.

82 Richard. L. Hughes and Katherine M. Beatty, *Becoming a Strategic Leader: Your Role in Your Organization's Enduring Success* (San Francisco: Jossey-Bass, 2005), 207–215.

83 O'Neill, *Executive Coaching with Backbone and Heart,* 2430.

84 Collins, *Christian Coaching,* 1038–1043.

85 Tony Stoltzfus, *Leadership Coaching: The Disciplines, Skills, and Heart of a Christian Coach* (Virginia Beach, VA: Tony Stoltzfus, 2005), 81–85.

86 Dave Ulrich, "Coaching for results," *Business Strategy Series* 9, no.3 (2008), 104–114, doi:10.1108/17515630810873320.

87 International Coach Federation, "Benefits of Using a Coach," International Coach Federation (ICF), http://www.coachfederation.org/need/landing.cfm?ItemNumber=747&navItemNumber=565.

Organizational Development

Organizational Development

EVERY LEADER MUST be able to lead their organization to new heights as well as grow and develop future leaders for organizational sustainability and growth. This requires strategic leadership skills and an organizational culture that is conducive to learning. While much of this information is based on organizational leadership research, theory, and best practices, it is still very applicable to apostolic church leaders. This module identifies several strategies to help leaders hone their organizational leadership skills and develop a vibrant, growing church.

CHAPTER 14

Strategic Leadership

EVERY ORGANIZATION IS affected by change. This change will either positively or negatively affect the organization. Adaptation to environmental change is imperative as organizations of all kinds, including churches, are operating in increasingly complex situations. This process of adaptation is strongly subjective to the interpretations that strategic leaders make of the surroundings, and that plays a huge role in organizations maintaining their effectiveness. What this means for church leaders is that the conditions both within the church and without are constantly changing. Thus, leaders must find the best methods to adapt to change, whether that entails implementing a new program, a new way of doing things, or teaching saints why the church will remain steadfast in its position regardless of how others change.

For example, at the present time, many churches are facing the decision to change the traditional service times and incorporating online services to reach a wider audience. This is a very good example of how church leaders make strategic decisions to aid in organizational development. For some churches, this may be a great solution or adjustment, but for others, it may be detrimental. This is why it is vital that every decision is backed with prayer and obedience regardless of what others are doing.

The fact is in order for an organization to create a viable future, leadership must have the ability to foresee, maintain flexibility, envision, think strategically, and work with others to create the necessary changes that are vital for success.

Leaders must possess the necessary skills to make the best decisions and implement the most effective plans for organizational success and sustainability. These skills include the ability to strategically think, act, and influence. It entails a learning process of creation, implementation, evaluation, and revision.[1] In other words, it involves the capability to create innovative ideas or processes, put action behind the thoughts, assess what is working, and make revisions as necessary.

The focus of strategic leadership is sustaining competitive advantage, which involves thinking, acting, and influencing in ways that ensure the success of an organization. Competitive advantage as a business term refers to an advantage over competitors by offering customers greater value, usually by means of lower prices or better services. Proverbs 23:23 states, "Buy the truth, and sell it not." Freely we have received, and we should freely give (Matthew 10:8). As the body of Christ, we are offering people a gift that is more valuable than anything this world could ever offer—the gospel of Jesus Christ. This is our competitive advantage, but how we are going to share the message requires strategic leadership.

Strategic thinking involves the gathering, creation, and evaluation of ideas and information that develop the organization's competitive advantage. It encompasses both the analytical techniques and tools such as measuring the important things that will provide information to effectively inform strategic decisions and ultimately give your church a competitive advantage, as well as developing vision, values, strategy, and organizational culture. For example, this process involves thinking through decisions that need to be made and is typically conducted as a brainstorming or planning meeting with church leaders. Where are we currently as a church? Are we fulfilling our mission? Are we reaching our goals? It is not enough to just talk about it; there needs to be some action that follows.

Strategic action is translating and prioritizing the strategic thoughts into action. What are we going to do to address this issue or take advantage of this opportunity? Furthermore, strategic planning involves setting priorities, strengthening operations, focusing energy and resources, ensuring common organization goals, and assessing the organization's direction in response to the changing environment.[2] How are we going to reach this goal? Who is doing what and by when?

These skills are necessary not only for senior leaders who are making organizational decisions but also leaders throughout the church, such as those who oversee specific departments. Let's take a look at an example of how a youth leader may apply the strategic leadership skills of thinking, acting, and planning.

————

Case Study

Mark is the youth pastor for a local assembly and has been for several years. Since taking this position, he has noticed that the youth tend to go on what he calls "spiritual roller coaster rides." There are times when the students seem on fire for God, and then there are months when they don't. Mark plans a youth staff meeting to see if others have the same perspective and if so, to find ways to address the issue. The youth staff meets, and Mark presents what has been on his mind and opens it up for discussion. The team agrees that for several months, the youth are excited and zealous toward God, and this is followed by periods of apathy. The leaders are also able to pinpoint when those times occur. To their surprise, the students were most zealous after conferences, fellowships, and other spiritual activities. They tended to lose momentum when there was not a lot going on with the group {the youth leaders are in Strategic Thinking mode}. They decide that something must be done to combat these spiritual lulls, so they make a list of things they could do that may help {Strategic Action}. After looking at the calendar, they realized there were several months without any kind of activity. Thus, they devised a plan to incorporate more things to keep the students involved {Strategic Planning}. They decided to research to see if there were any other youth conferences or retreats already planned that they could attend, assigning each person this task to follow up on within the next two weeks. They also decided to have Mark ask the pastor if they could add a couple more youth-oriented services and prayer meetings to the calendar each month. Finally, they added some more fun activities to keep the students connected. They decided that once a month, they would have fellowship and go out or go to someone's place to hang out as a group. Then, twice a year, they would plan a big activity such as a retreat or trip. They talked about who was going to be responsible for what specific items and which activities they all would plan together. They also scheduled some follow-up meetings just to touch base to see if things were going according to plan. They left the meeting exhilarated, knowing they had in place a great plan to address the issue that would not be too taxing on any single individual or the student's pocketbook, but most importantly, would hopefully help resolve the issue.

As you can tell from the case study, strategy making is about people creating outcomes.[3] However, it is crucial that values, goals, and strategy align in order to achieve the church's vision. Vision provides the motivation to work toward a common purpose, but strategy links action to vision. In other words, leaders of departments should keep in mind the overarching vision and mission of the church and how their actions align with each. Alignment between leadership, strategy, and culture is crucial to organizational effectiveness.[4] Thus, competitive advantage (i.e., propagating the gospel) and overall organizational (church) effectiveness are influenced by leadership's ability to align the missions, goals, and strategies, and to find the fit between internal strengths and externalities (the external environment) in the world. Leaders who possess strategic thinking, acting, and planning skills are vital for successful organizational effectiveness.

———

There are specific competencies that leaders can develop to help them think more strategically. These include:[5]

- **Assessing**: Assessing where the organization is currently. This involves examining the strengths and weaknesses inside the church as well as the threats and opportunities in the environment (e.g., SWOT analysis).
- **Visioning**: A view of what the church is and what it should become. It involves knowing the aspirations, core values, and culture of your church and where God wants it to be in the future.
- **Reframing**: Looking at things from a different perspective. This requires restating or questioning the implicit beliefs that are often taken for granted by members and having the ability to view and think about things differently. For example, what could we do differently if we listened to team members? What could we be the best at? What are some different ways to think about what quality means in our church?
- **Systems Thinking**: Discerning the relationships among different variables in complex circumstances. This requires tactics such as looking for patterns over time, looking for complex interactions, looking at the big picture, understanding what causes what, and postulating causal relationships. How does my department affect the whole church?
- **Making Common Sense**: Examining how others view things. This involves helping others in the church make sense of things and not assuming that one person's perspective is correct. It requires having a shared understanding of ideas, values, and goals.

CHAPTER 15

Organizational Culture

CULTURE IS EMBEDDED within the organization and is what makes every church unique. Organizational culture is the shared beliefs and values that influence people's behavior.[6] These basic assumptions are taught, whether implicitly or explicitly, to new members as the way to think, perceive, and feel in an organization.[7] Culture also influences the processes and outcomes that the church hopes to achieve. For example, how friendly church members are, the color schemes and building design, how people interact, and how services and meetings are conducted all make up the culture. There are many forces that shape a church's culture, however, pastors and senior leaders typically have the most influence. The most prominent reason for this is because leaders shape the direction of the church.

It is important for church leaders to create a culture that is consistent with their vision, mission, and values. The primary goal of the church is to seek and save the lost (Matthew 18:12, 28:18–20). Thus, every church should have a culture that is welcoming. The attitudes and actions of members should reflect the love of Christ. The building should be comfortable and have enough room for people to sit. It needs to be clean, both inside and out, as this also reflects on the culture of the church. It sends an implicit message that this church cares! We want the lost to know we care and they can find hope here. While every church may have different budgets, we all have the capacity to be good stewards and take care of the things we have as well as develop a culture conducive to evangelism.

Cultural Conflict

In some instances, leaders may not be aware of their own emotional issues or conflicts, and thus may be sending mutually conflicting messages that lead to a varying degree of culture conflict.[8] Church culture mirrors and responds to the behaviors, patterns, prejudices, and choices of leaders. Subordinate anxiety and eventually weakened organizational effectiveness will occur. This leadership inconsistency will cause followers to rely on their own experience or other signals, leading to a much more diverse set of assumptions and subcultures.

For example, most churches have handbooks they get members to sign if they want to be part of a group that is on the platform, such as the music team or choir. It may be tempting for music directors to overlook or ignore members who are not being submissive to the handbook. Perhaps that person has a really great talent or they are really close friends with the music director's family. Maybe the leader does not feel it is a big issue and shouldn't be in the handbook to begin with, so they passively pretend to not notice or they ignore the issue. This can cause conflict as others most likely realize it too and see how it is being handled, consequently sending a conflicting message and creating diverse assumptions about some of the aspects of the culture.

Ultimately, people should keep their eyes off of others and look to Jesus. However, human tendencies are to question the overall culture—does it include obedience or something else? Thus, to avoid this type of culture conflict, what leaders most often pay attention to, control, reward, react to, and communicate should reflect and be consistent with the assumptions, values, and goals of the church. In addition to leaders sending conflicting messages, another inconsistency that can cause cultural conflict is when leaders' values do not align with the organization's culture.

The leaders' values should align with the overall desire for the organizational culture, as inconsistency will cause cultural problems like in the music director example. The leader's success will depend to a large extent on their knowledge and understanding of the organizational culture. For example, a newly elected pastor cannot go into a church and dramatically change the way things are done, such as what type of music is played, without some resistance. It is important for leaders to understand the culture, establish what type is needed for the organization, and then shape it to match the ideal culture.[9]

A leader will spend much of his or her time with the forces that shape the values and attitudes of followers at all levels. Thus, leaders begin the culture creation process, manage it, and even change it when necessary. Problems arise when leaders do not have the ability to manage culture effectively. A misunderstanding of the leader's own perspective or knowledge of organizational culture often causes this. One way to combat this issue is for the leader to learn more about themselves and the organizational culture. Effective leaders will model the way by clarifying their own values, affirming shared values, and aligning their actions with those shared values.[10] The most effective leaders are continuously striving to grow, learning more about themselves and effectively communicating the goals of the organization. Following are some tips to avoid cultural conflict and create a consistent and congruent church culture.

Tips for Cultural Congruency

It is essential that leaders understand themselves and the organization's culture, as success depends on it.[11] In order to manage organizational culture, one must first understand the culture and then use that information to help guide one's own behaviors as well as the group's behavior. There are several assessments that can assist leaders in understanding both their values and the organizational culture, including the organizational cultural assessment inventory (OCAI) and other 360-degree assessments. The OCAI is designed to assess current culture as well as identify a preferred future culture.[12] These are typically used for business organizations but can be tailored for churches. A consultant or coach can assist with the implementation of these assessments as well as provide advice on how to use the results to assist with organizational change.

Here are some tips to aid in cultural congruency:

- Identify the current culture and compare it to the preferred culture.
- Engage staff who align with the culture.
- Communicate the culture.
- Address cultural conflicts.

Leaders and the groups they manage tend to be more successful when the leadership strengths are congruent with the dominant organizational culture. Therefore, since culture is ultimately created, evolved, and changed by leaders, it is important that the leaders' and organization's values align in addition to leaders having a consistent message. Equally important is creating a learning environment that supports innovation and developing visionary leaders.

CHAPTER 16

Innovation and Foresight

Being innovative and productive is one key to an organization's success. Leaders must possess the foresight necessary to propel the organization forward and remain successful. Thus, it is not enough for leaders to have an idea or vision, they must be willing to put forth the time and effort to see the goals come to fruition. Just like the virtuous woman in Proverbs 31, who did not have idle hands and was willing to work productively throughout the night, creating fine linens to sell in addition to taking care of her household responsibilities (Proverbs 31:15, 24, and 27). Additionally, it is not enough to possess innovative ideas, as leaders should work to close the "knowing–doing gap" by putting actions behind the knowledge.[13]

Innovative leaders think and act differently than others, which ultimately makes a difference in their success. The most effective innovative church leaders regularly ask thought-provoking questions, experiment to find novel solutions, network with a diverse group of people, and connect insights to new ideas. They are continuously striving to find new methods to connect to people and lead them closer to Christ. Additionally, they are good stewards with their resources.

Stewardship

In order for the church to continuously grow, leaders must learn to be good stewards of resources. Stewardship is a biblical concept that entails the responsible planning and management of resources. This applies within the church, our homes, work, and every other aspect of life. 1 Corinthians 4:2 tells us that it is required in stewards for a man to be found faithful. Ultimately, God owns everything, and we are merely the stewards tasked with making the most of His resources. We can just keep His resources that He has given us, or we can be innovative and creative and multiply them for His glory, just as the faithful servants did in the parable of the talents (Matthew 25:14–30).

Here again, the virtuous woman in Proverbs 31 provides a good example of biblical stewardship. She considers the field before she purchases it to make sure she is making a wise investment and investing her profits in the future (Proverbs 31:16). She produces quality goods and services and has a global mindset, importing and exporting goods in the global market (Proverbs 31:14, 22, and 24).[14] Further, she gives of her resources to help those in need (Proverbs 31:20). Successful leaders find ways to make the most of their resources, while taking care of their family needs and continuously improving to meet the needs of the church.[15] Thus, if innovative leaders intend to be successful, they must wisely invest their time and resources as well as develop a learning culture to continue church growth and success.

Learning Culture

Alignment between leadership, strategy, and culture is crucial to organizational effectiveness. Therefore, it is vital for churches to have a culture of learning and growth if any leader development is to be effective. Developing a leadership culture is about growing leadership talent to the needed level of capability.[16] However, it takes more than just casting a vision and providing training to produce a learning organization. There are at least three other building blocks for learning organizations, which can easily be remembered by the acronym CAR:[17]

- Concrete learning processes
- A supportive learning environment
- Reinforcement from leadership

In other words, learning needs to be built into the culture of the organization. Organizations should demonstrate the value of formal and informal learning, reward and promote expertise, and allow people to make mistakes.[18] Developing a learning organization is a process that leaders should continuously strive to improve in order to progress in the midst of change.

Additionally, leader development must be supported throughout the organization through values, culture, mindset, and behaviors of existing leaders.[19] Culture must be aligned with and supportive of church strategy in order for it to be successful. Both teamwork and leadership development are key factors to organizational effectiveness, particularly if their attributes fit the sociocultural context.[20] Thus, for successful development to occur, a church leader must be willing to learn to see the world through diverse cultural lenses so they can perceive and decipher the cultural forces that operate in groups.

Teaching

Often, teaching is a method used to help people learn and grow. Both leaders and non-aspiring leaders should be taught. Leaders are often responsible for teaching others the Word of God. However, it is equally important that non-leaders also have the skills to teach, as teaching is a powerful outreach tool. Bible studies are simple and effective resources that can help win people to God. They will also help ground the teacher in the Word because they will be studying the Bible themselves. 1 Timothy 3:16 encourages us to study to show ourselves approved unto God.

When teaching, it is important to incorporate various styles, particularly when teaching a large class, such as Sunday school. Every person learns by one or a combination of various methods, such as hearing, seeing, reading, or doing. You may want to have people read Bible passages, incorporate a related video or activity, tell a story, or have group discussions. It is also important to mix things up and not do things the same way every time, to keep people interested and anticipating what they will be doing and learning in class. By incorporating various methods, you will be able to reach a larger audience, and the subject will be more likely to be retained. Moreover, teaching is also one of the best forms of outreach and assimilation.

CHAPTER 17

Outreach and Visitor Retention and Assimilation

SCRIPTURE TEACHES THE main purpose of the church is to evangelize the world (Mark 16:15; Acts 1:8). Jesus commanded that the church would preach the gospel, drawing all mankind to God (Matthew 28:19). Thus, a spiritual leadership priority should be church growth as it is a measure of how successful the church is at fulfilling the Great Commission.[21]

Fulfilling the Great Commission is vital for the growth and success of the apostolic church because it is a foundational doctrinal point and is also the means through which people are converted to Christ. However, many churches have put a priority on numbers only rather than evangelism, but often, those churches only interested in acquiring a number will lack the love and spirit necessary to sustain growth.[22]

While outreach is imperative, it is equally important to retain and develop those people the church reaches for Christ.[23] This can be equated to a recruiting process that organizations undertake to find people who will work toward their desired goal. For businesses, this means accepting résumés, conducting interviews, and finding the right person–job fit. However, for the church, there is only one requirement: "whosoever will." Therefore, the church leader's skill set should include outreach and visitor retention techniques. This does not mean the answer is to reduce the task of reaching the lost to a certain set of processes and procedures. However, it does require church leaders to be able to devise a specific action plan that will reach their community. For example, how does the church invite guests? Do you use marketing techniques via websites, social media, word of mouth, social gatherings, or community outreach? Next, how do you treat visitors when they do attend? What methods do you use to get them to return? How do you get these people involved in the church?

All of these things should be considered and included in the church's strategic action plan along with the overall vision and mission of the church.

Mission and Vision

Vision and foresight are vital in church leadership. As previously discussed, Christians were given the ultimate vision of God's strategic plan during the Great Commission. However, we should not be so naïve as to believe it will fulfill itself. It takes all of us working together, and we may have various ways of fulfilling the mission. Some people confuse mission and vision because they are so closely related, but mission has to do with goals and purpose, and vision is the unprecedented destination that your church is constantly working toward. Thus, a specific vision and its relationship to your mission must be created and communicated repeatedly. Repeating the vision keeps what is important in the forefront of followers' minds. The mission should also be communicated often. You can communicate it in several ways, such as on a website, in handbooks, on banners, and in classes. This not only keeps people connected to the mission of the church but also keeps in the forefront of their mind where they are headed, thus keeping the whole church in one mind and one accord.

Motivating Volunteers

One of the most challenging aspects of being a leader is finding ways to motivate volunteers. First and foremost, it has to be in the person's heart to do a particular job. They need to be able to relate their job to the bigger picture, which is the mission. For example, a student who helps a Sunday school teacher get the room set up or makes coffee for a group Bible Study are completing important tasks that many times helps relieve the leader to focus on their job of teaching. We find the apostles did the same thing in Acts 6. They had duties that were being overlooked, and they needed to be able to focus on their job, so they had others appointed for those tasks. Likewise, leaders today need help and have volunteers, but it can be challenging to keep people motivated, especially when they are not getting paid.

However, there are a few strategies that can help keep volunteers motivated.

1. ***Align with the Mission***: Volunteer jobs must reflect the importance of the overall mission and vision of the church. This needs to be communicated to the volunteer, and perhaps demonstrated, so they can understand their important role. Using the same example of the student who makes coffee before Bible Study, the volunteer may feel like it is an insignificant role, as many times, people want to jump right to the top and be the teacher. However, they may still need to be developed in the Word and maybe other areas as well. It is a process. Some people are already equipped with great talents and gifts, and they just need a little guidance or perhaps to demonstrate they are committed to the cause. Either way, they must understand how their simple task of making coffee is helping the visitors feel welcomed and comfortable. The overall goal is to reach this soul, and they are doing their part, as well as demonstrating a servant's heart.

   Every job is important in the Kingdom, and we must be careful not to place emphasis on certain roles all the time. This may breed volunteers who only want to get to the position where they then think they have arrived at spiritual maturity, or whatever. However, this is not the right motive. By helping people understand their importance in the church and how it aligns with the overall mission, you give them a sense of ownership, community, and commitment to the cause. This is exactly what we should desire; everyone in the body doing his or her part to make it work as it is designed (Ephesians 4:16). Not every person is called to preach, teach, or sing. However, as leaders, we should still help everyone find their work for the Lord.

2. ***Find the Right Person–Job Fit***: This refers to matching volunteers' knowledge, skills, and abilities to specific job-related tasks in the work environment. It further describes the relationship between the types of tasks a person performs on the job and their personality.[24] Volunteers must have the skills, personality, and capability, or at least the capacity, to learn a job before they can do it. This will require the leader to invest a little time to train, but it will be an enriching experience for both parties. The leader will learn skills for being a better leader, including how to teach and how to relate to people, while the volunteer will learn a new ministry as well as see how leadership is modeled from their mentor.

3. ***Encourage, Support, and Thank***: It is vital that volunteers feel appreciated, are encouraged, and have the support they need to do their job. Feedback from leaders is crucial to helping volunteers stay committed. Otherwise, they will have no idea if they are correctly fulfilling their duties or doing a good job.

We know many times, leaders will complain or get frustrated with volunteers, but they have never sat down with them to talk about the issues. In some cases, they never even identified the volunteer's role. They may say, "We need you to do such and such," but without further instruction, the volunteers are left to figure things out on their own. If this is what you intend, then great, but do not complain if it is not done the way you would have done it or the way you wanted it done. On the other hand, giving volunteers the freedom to do their job in a creative way helps to keep them motivated, as they see it as *their* project.

Thus, the best approach, when possible, is to give general guidelines such as the end goal and then allow the volunteer to arrive at the goal in their own manner. If things need to be done a certain way on a few tasks, then give them the instructions so that they can do a good job unto the Lord. If you see a volunteer getting discouraged or lax, encourage them and remind them how important their role is in the Kingdom and to the mission. Talk with them to find out if there is anything they need. Effective communication is crucial to keeping volunteers motivated. Also, do not forget to thank them for their help. Everyone likes to be appreciated.

CHAPTER 18

Conflict and Change

IN A WORLD of constant turmoil and change, apostolic leaders must be equipped to effectively deal with change and conflict.

Managing Conflict

Unfortunately, there will be times when leaders must deal with conflict. Sometimes it is between the leader and a follower, and other times, it may be between two members, or even a member and a visitor. A leader must use wisdom when dealing with conflict and be able to listen to both sides without preconceived ideas. Matthew 18:15–17 tells us how to deal with conflict, stating that if a brother sins against you, you should go point out the fault between the two of you. If he listens, then you have won him over, or in other words, resolved the conflict. If he chooses not to listen, then take with you two or three witnesses that every word be established. If the person still refuses to listen, then tell it to the church. Finally, if he will not listen to the church, then let him be as a heathen to you.

There are some very straightforward steps identified that leaders should teach for how to deal with conflict. We want people to grow in Christ, and in order to do so, they must know how to deal with conflict. We are all humans and have to deal with this fleshly nature. Thus, a church should establish how they will deal with conflict when it arises and should then teach it to members. This will help them learn how to resolve conflict among themselves, which is a great life skill. It will also allow followers to understand what to do if such a circumstance arises.

We always recommend beginning with prayer. When we begin with prayer, we allow God to speak to our hearts and to get our spirits right. Before addressing a person or issue, it is important to examine ourselves. Often, we find it was our own attitude, jealousy, or issue that caused us to perceive something that may not have been there. On the other hand, the Holy Ghost may prompt us to just pray for that person and not approach them at all. We never know what someone may be already dealing with that could influence the way they act. Here is an example of a conflict resolution process.

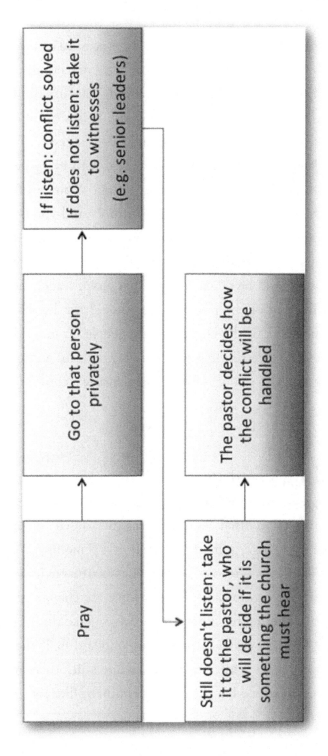

Of course, your conflict resolution process may differ. It also greatly depends on what type of conflict. For example, a simple miscommunication or misunderstanding can usually be easily resolved within just the first two steps. It is a beautiful thing when people learn how to communicate and resolve problems. It also keeps leaders from having to deal with every petty little issue, which can be very time-consuming. Who cares that Sis. Dessert took a peach cobbler to the dinner and you wanted an apple cobbler. I know this is humorous, but you can probably think of several situations like this fairly quickly. However, bigger issues should be taken straight to a senior leader such as department head or the pastor. Issues should not be shared with other members of the church to get people on one side or the other, as this breeds division. This is why our outline always shows going to a senior leader to help resolve a conflict.

Leading Change

Although we examine leading change as an individual leadership skill, this section discusses it in an organizational context. Some people love change, and others hate it. It is sometimes something that is just built into our personalities or the environments in which we are comfortable. Some people are change agents and are always looking for innovative ways to make things improve. Others will wait to see if people are onboard or if there seems to be any results with the change, while still others will resist change no matter what the case. All humans like consistency to some extent, as it makes us feel safe and in our element. Thus, leading a change initiative at church can sometimes be challenging. Whether we are talking about a minor change like decorating a class or something more major like changing the format of our services or building, there are several strategies to help leaders implement change. These include:

- Link the change to the mission and vision.
- Develop a strategic change action plan.
  - What is the goal?
  - How will we reach it?
  - What do we need?
  - How will we know it works?
- Communicate the change.
  - Why is it important?
  - What will it entail?
  - How will we get there?
  - What are the results?
- Allow people time to adjust and mentally prepare for it, especially with big changes.

This is particularly true when you begin to change positions or implement new ones, as some people may get uncomfortable or even territorial. Their feelings may get hurt, as if their role is being taken over by someone else, or they may feel that they are not doing a good enough job. The enemy loves to move into these situations to cause division and lies. This is why communication is so vital! It is always best to talk with that person, listen to their concerns, and help them see the reason behind the change that is linked to the overall vision. Additionally, pastors and senior leaders must support the change and model the way. It is not enough to tell people about an upcoming change, the leader must be willing to support the change initiative throughout the entire process and provide followers whatever resources necessary to implement the change.

CHAPTER 19

Teams

CHURCHES SHOULD SEEK a balance between developing individual leaders' competencies and fostering the collective capabilities of groups, teams, and organizational leadership. This entails developing others, creating diverse and effective teams including talent identification and management, and ministry creation and placement.

Develop Others

Authentic leadership is morally grounded, transparent, and responsive to the values and needs of those they lead.[25] A leader's main concern should be the church's overall well-being as the body of Christ.[26] Followers have a tremendous impact on a church's performance, growth, and overall effectiveness. However, a leader's main focus should not be about numbers or money, but about the people. Thus, it is very important to spend time developing them.

All throughout the Bible, we see scriptures of leaders developing followers. Jesus demonstrated a great example in developing His followers. He spent time with them (Luke 10:38–42), taught them (Matthew 13), loved them (John 19:26), and served them (John 13:1–17). Excellent leadership requires meaningful relationships with followers. There are many leaders who just lead and do not strive to develop relationships with people or help develop them. This is one of the biggest hindrances to church growth.

Just as employees want more out of a job than high pay and good salaries, people want more from their leaders than the capability to teach a good class or preach a good sermon, even though these are necessary traits. Followers want and need their leaders to think about their personal development. They too desire to work for a leader they can respect and who cares for them.[27] Of course, one leader cannot invest in every follower, especially in churches of hundreds or thousands. This is why teams and team leaders are vital to the health of a church. It helps to close the gap of people feeling lost, unimportant, or lonely, as they have someone to lead, connect with, and mentor them more frequently than a pastor may be able to in a large congregation. On the other hand, it does not excuse senior leaders or pastors from having any relationships with followers. They must also invest in relationships, especially with their other leaders, to help them grow and pour into their teams. Investing in the development of followers will bring about greater motivation, satisfaction, and organizational success.

Diverse Teams

Churches must also have diverse teams to be able to reach a multitude of people. Paul provides a great example of the importance of diverse teams and how to build them. Although Paul still faced communication and social challenges, he developed a diverse team that enabled him to have an effective cross-cultural ministry. They understood how cultural norms shaped society and looked for commonalities as a reference point to begin the conversation of conversion, all the while sharing a common Christian social identity among the team of believers.

Churches need to develop this same strategy to reach the vast majority of people and fulfill its prime mandate. They must not only understand the culture, they must also know how to best communicate and relate to the people in the region. Perceptibly, followers who are already familiar with a particular culture are best suited to effectively work with, collaborate with, and lead within the community. However, the church still needs to define its own cultural norms and how it operates, such as value systems that will transform into a good cross-cultural fit. They must assess cultural norms to ensure there is a suitable fit for moving forward culturally, environmentally, and politically. If there is not a good fit, the key is to devise a strategy that will allow the church to optimally collaborate and reach out without losing its own values.

Working in diverse churches can be challenging, but when done collaboratively, it can be very beneficial. Among the several benefits of diverse are more and greater diversity of resources, larger pool of knowledge and expertise, and collective creation.[28] Diversity in churches is highly valued, as it creates an organizational culture that broadens opportunities for leaders and members. Diversity helps followers develop in new ways by putting people in positions to stretch their current skill sets and perceptions, which also helps to build their capabilities and cultural agility.[29] However, there are also challenges especially associated with communication. Cross-cultural communications increase the chance for misinterpretation because people interpret and act through their own cultural perspectives.[30] Therefore, leaders must strengthen their communication skills to accurately interpret and respond appropriately to diversity.

Building Effective Teams

Teamwork is another area of concern within the organizational development of a church. Leaders should be able to develop highly productive and visionary teams in order to enhance effectiveness.[31] Teams should not be confused with groups, as while there are many similarities between the two, there are also many differences. They are both a collective body of individuals, however, groups refer to a collection of people who cooperate with one another and work toward a common purpose though there is a difference in their individual accountability.[32] Although teams are a type of group, they display collective accountability as opposed to a group's individual accountability. Effective teams operate to build shared commitment, task-appropriate coordination, and collective skills.[33] An example of a group is a Bible study group. A team may be your student ministry leader team that works toward planning activities and developing young people.

A team that hopes to be effective must push past the norm, continually growing and striving for excellence. This level of commitment takes place at both an individual and group level. It is the leader's job to manage the team and make sure that any ulterior motives are kept in check. If some members strive only to accomplish personal goals and ambitions, then the team as a whole will suffer, becoming unproductive and inefficient. However, the overall performance and effectiveness of the team can and will exceed the sum of its parts when every member strives to be better than they were before.

Moreover, every member of the team must be united for a team to be effective. Nehemiah is remembered for his leadership ability in rebuilding the walls of Jerusalem. However, he would not have been nearly as successful without the determination and unity of the people who worked under him. Nehemiah 4:6 states, "So built we the wall; and all the wall was joined together unto the half thereof: for the people had a mind to work." Just as it was a collective effort for Nehemiah and his team, so should it be in the twenty-first century apostolic church. But remember, a team can only be as productive as the one who leads it.

Talent Identification and Management

Helping people discover their talent and potential is essential to being an effective leader and is part of the discernment construct of the servant leadership model. A church that understands the power of collaboration will make growing and developing people a top priority. There must be a definite calling and talent already evident when it comes to appointing leaders in the church (1

Timothy 3). Additionally, aspiring leaders should already have a good grasp on spiritual disciplines as this is the foundation for all spiritual leadership. Then, individuals' callings and talents must be identified and developed by the existing leadership in order to create effective successive leadership in the church.

When individuals are placed in positions that are not a good spiritual and physical fit, it will lead to ineffectiveness, low morale, and burnout. One of the best ways to determine if people are a good fit is by understanding their interests and God-given talents, personality, and gifts. This requires self-awareness as well as spiritual insight. Some people learn by doing, so it may also be a good idea to allow people to try out certain ministries for a short time without having to commit to a long-term position. If people know up front they can try a ministry, they may be more apt to volunteer, realizing they will not create a big problem for the church if they decide the position is not a good fit for them. This may also provide the church with a larger pool of volunteers, allowing people to rotate positions.

Ministry Creation and Placement

When people are saved and born into the Kingdom, it is up to leaders to help them grow and find their place in God. Every person is unique and has gifts allocated to them by God. As leaders, we can help them discover those gifts and teach them to be good stewards. The talents parable is a great example of how God feels about those who do not use and multiply their gifts for

His glory. There are so many members of each church who just come and sit on the pew every service because they are not teachers, singers, or preachers, so they do not know what they can do. Sure, these are all needed areas, but at times, there may be too much emphasis on these and not enough on others.

Members cannot get involved if they do not know what they can do. This applies both inside and outside of the church. Followers need to have an understanding that their gifts can be used both inside the church building and out in the marketplace. For example, a seamstress may have a business where they provide goods and services to customers, provide jobs, are able to be a good witness and financially bless the church. They may also help sew church costumes or robes when needed. This is an example of how someone can use their gifts in both manners.

However, many times, people separate the two completely. There may be chefs, lawyers, real estate professionals, business owners, accountants, nurses, teachers, doctors, and other professionals just sitting on the pews thinking their services are not needed. God placed them in the church to build the body and help others. We are the body of Christ, and we each have an important part in the Kingdom (1 Corinthians 12:27).

Here are some practical steps for leaders to help others find their ministry:

1. Teach others about gifts and callings and how they are used both inside and outside the church.
2. Help them discover their true passion and gifts.
3. Show them places they can use their gifts.

185

4. Create opportunities to utilize gifts.
5. Work with others to help develop their gifts.

A church that focuses on developing others, teaching them how to use their gifts to fulfill the mission of Christ, will grow into a vibrant, healthy body! There will be more unity and fulfillment in God.

CHAPTER 20

Pastoral Authority and Church Structure

ALTHOUGH MINISTRY PLACEMENT should be left to the pastor of a church, it is still imperative that church leaders understand this process. This is particularly true for those leaders beginning new ministries or starting new churches. Each pastor will have his own church structure and process of placing people in ministry. However, many churches have a similar structure such as outreach, Sunday school, youth, ushers and greeters, and other small groups or supports. For this reason, this section is purposely left generalized for each church to discuss their specific church structure and its processes. This will ensure that every leader has an understanding and is on the same page. In addition to explaining church structure, there are several things to consider, including: What types of ministries your church will have. How do you determine who is the right fit for that ministry? What does a person do if they need a break, want to resign a position, or move to another ministry? How long does a person serve in a particular role?

These are all great topics to discuss with leaders, as it helps to build unity in the church, but one of the most important factors to include is submission.

Submission

Submission is one of those topics that some people get uncomfortable talking about, yet it is critical for effective church ministries and growth. Submission is easy when all of our hearts are pure and we have the right motives. For clarity, we are not referring to being submissive to abusive leaders or those unrepentantly living in sin, as they should be confronted and removed from office (1 Timothy 5:19–21). Leaders should not be ruling with an iron fist to feed their ego or pride, but should be striving to be godly leaders (1 Peter 5:3–11; 2 Corinthians 1:24).

Likewise, followers should not be rebellious, selfish, or desire that everything be done their way. Hebrews 13:17 states, "Have confidence in your leaders and submit to their authority, because they keep watch over you as those who must give an account. Do this so that their work will be a joy, not a burden, for that would be of no benefit to you" (NIV).

There may be times as a follower when you question your leaders' actions. This is not the time to get an attitude or stir up strife in the church, as the scripture specifically speaks against such actions (Proverbs 15:18; 2 Timothy 2:22–26). The conflict resolution model is still applicable in this situation, so first, you must pray. Pray for your leader as well as yourself. Make sure your motives are pure and that you are in sync with God and not what the flesh desires. The Lord will speak through your pastor as this is the way He designed spiritual authority (Acts 20:28; 1 Peter 5:1–4; 1 Thessalonians 5:12–13). This is why it is so important that we pray for our pastors and leaders. They need to hear from God and have the vision for the church. If you still have a concern, then go to the leader to get understanding and share your thoughts. This may provide a new perspective for the leader to pray about and seek God's direction.

Ultimately, followers should obey the direction of their godly leader. God will deal with that person's heart if they need it, but it may just be a test of obedience for you. Remember, to obey is better than sacrifice and rebellion, and stubbornness is as the sin of witchcraft, idolatry, and iniquity (1 Samuel 15:22–23). God forbid our hearts become impure because we do not agree with certain decisions or actions of a leader or our pastor!

Pray for all men, pray for our leaders (1 Timothy 2:1–3). Our pastor must oversee and give an account to the Lord for us and of their stewardship (Acts 20:28; Hebrews 13:7; 1 Peter 5:1–4). It is best to esteem our leaders, give honor to whom it is due, and treat them the way we would like to be treated if we were in their position (1 Thessalonians 5:12–13; Romans 13:7). Pastors have a heavy burden on them to care for the souls of the saints. At times, there are a lot of needs and pressures from dealing with people, things in the church, and their own personal life. We should not be so quick to judge or put unnecessary pressure on their family to be perfect. After all, they are humans too and have to deal with the same flesh that we do. However, we should love, encourage, and support our leaders to the best of our ability and unto the Lord, so that they can effectively lead us closer to God's vision. The Lord will reward our obedience, bring unity to the church, and bless it to flourish!

CHAPTER 21

Systems

THERE IS MUCH debate among church leaders concerning systems and processes. Some say systematizing things emphasizes too much of man's ways and does not leave room for God to work, while others advocate for them, having implemented them and experienced growth. Often, people do not realize they already have systems in place because they do not think of them in those terms. For example, does your church have different departments with specific functions? Do you have a certain method or outline for services? Do you have a process for new guests? This is all part of a system. However, with every service, you still allow God to take control or interrupt things at any given time. This is the way it should be, as it is all about God and reaching souls.

God likes systems and processes. Being born again is a process beginning with repentance, baptism, and infilling of the gift of the Holy Ghost that so perfectly aligns with the death, burial, and resurrection of Christ. Then, there is a process that takes time, developing and maturing in Christ (1 Corinthians 3:12; Hebrews 5:12; 1 Peter 2:2). Also think about the way God designed the human body. We are full of systems such as the cardiovascular, respiratory, and digestive systems. Jesus used an analogy of the body to describe how the body of Christ should function (1 Corinthians 12:12). In fact, 1 Corinthians 14:40 tells us that everything should be done decently and in order.

There are many examples of successful systems in the Bible, most notably Nehemiah and Noah. God gave a command, and they did not just throw things together. Instead, they had a plan and process for how they would achieve their goals. Likewise, every church should have a plan to reach their desired God-given goals. That being said, every church is unique and should seek God for His direction, including on what systems should be in place. The most critical aspect to remember is that it all must be built upon the spiritual disciplines, continuously seeking God's direction, and allowing Him to move and change things as He pleases. In other words, we must not be so bent on systems and processes that we leave God out of the equation. We must always be on guard because with systems, people can tend to become lazy or rely upon habits or talents instead of God.

We will briefly discuss a couple of systems that we feel should be considered and included, such as a learning system, leadership development, and succession planning. We already discussed learning systems, and it can be reviewed in the Creating a Learning Culture section. To reiterate, since we are all growing in Christ, it is of utmost importance to have a method to cultivate that growth, for instance through exercising spiritual disciplines and having a means for people to learn the Word of God such as Bible studies and classes. Most churches already have these sorts of systems in place. However, it is important to continually assess whether or not they are being effective and fulfilling their intended purpose. If not, implement some type of change that will better align with the culture and vision.

Leadership Development Systems

One of the most vital aspects of a church, or any organization, is developing leaders. Unfortunately, it is often overlooked or taken for granted that people will naturally have these skills. Yes, it is true that some people are born with natural leadership abilities; however, most people, including those born with some innate talent for leadership, still need to work on developing these skills. The good news is that most leadership skills can be learned, and it is up to the church to develop godly people who will be capable of effectively leading others. This is where a leader development system can prove to be most beneficial.

A leader development system is broader than just a curriculum or development initiative; rather, it encompasses all aspects of the organization that contribute to producing effective leaders for the purpose of performance improvement, succession management, and organizational change.[34] Leader development systems are not a one size fits all approach, nor should they be. Every organization has its own set of goals, values, structure, and systems.[35] Organizations create models or frameworks to summarize the skills, knowledge, and perspectives that distinguish superior leadership performance and assess competencies that need to be developed in leaders.[36]

Organizations might adopt an existing model because it comes from a reputable source, begin with an existing model and then tailor it to align with organizational values and priorities, or create their own from scratch. For example, the Center for Creative Leadership developed a two-part conceptual framework for developing leaders, ACS and DAC, which has proven to be successful in a variety of contexts and cultures, including churches.[37] In the first part, assessments, challenges, and support (ACS) combine to make the developmental experience more powerful.[38] Assessments can play a vital role in identifying the current mindset concerning leadership development and where they would like to develop. The second model demonstrates that leader development is a process requiring a variety of developmental experiences and the capability to learn from those experiences.[39] DAC is composed of direction, alignment, and commitment.[40] The framework suggests that leadership does not exist without:

- *Direction*: A shared understanding of where the collective is going in regard to objectives, goals, and vision.
- *Alignment*: Effective collaboration, coordination, and communication.
- *Commitment*: Pursuing collective goals above individual goals.

Organizational consultants and leadership coaches can be useful for assisting with the design, implementation, and evaluation of leadership development initiatives that fit your church's needs.

Assessment instruments such as the Organizational Culture Assessment Instrument (OCAI) can assist with defining key behaviors and culture that are critical for organizational success.[41] Leader development systems should be vigorous, with developmental experiences such as feedback-intensive programs and coaching relationships that enhance learning and expose leaders to new knowledge, insights, and the acquisition of new skills. They should also align with the organizational goals and culture.[42] For example, an effective leadership development system will include things such as:

- A leadership development curriculum such as this one, aligned to the church's vision and goals.
- Examples of effective leadership modeled by senior leaders.
- Opportunities to develop leadership skills (e.g., experience).
- Assessments (personal and 360).
- Mentoring and coaching.
- Advice from pastors.

Each church will have their own system, tailored to meet their specific needs. Every leader should be aware of the process and implement it within their respective departments as a mean to develop future leaders, or it can be done as a collective group, depending on the size of the church. For further examples of specific methods of leadership development, please see that section. Moreover, it will take cultivating relationships, teams, and effective communication to ensure that any program is successful.

Succession Planning

Organizations must have capable leaders ready and willing to continue the success of the organization. What good will it do if you, as a leader, aspire and fulfill your vision but there is nobody there to sustain it or keep the church growing when you are gone? It can be scary at times to think about relinquishing control to someone, especially if it has been your "baby" from the beginning. However, God wants continual success and growth of the church. He wants your efforts and the fruit of your labor to continue to bring Him glory. If there is nobody to take up the mantle and take your place, things will eventually begin to deteriorate. Every program, process, system, and organization needs a leader in order to survive. This is true for the church as well; churches need pastors, leaders, and directors to continue to thrive.

Succession planning is a practice found in numerous places in the Bible, including Elijah and Elisha (2 Kings 2:11–14), Moses and Joshua (Deuteronomy 31:14–30), and Paul and Timothy (2 Timothy 4). Using the example of Paul and Timothy, Paul made sure that he had a successor to carry out the ministry. Succession planning is likened to a relay race, as it has to do with passing on responsibility; if you drop the baton, then you lose the race.[43] Paul understood that his "race" was coming to an end, but he already had his plans in place, and he was assuring that the baton would not be dropped.

However, it typically takes time for protégés to be developed as successors. Paul and Timothy traveled together as a team for many years.[44] They had become close friends, and Paul often called Timothy brother or son. For many years, Paul invested in Timothy, and at the end of his life, he needed Timothy to come minister to him (2 Timothy 4:9–21). There comes a time when leaders need the support of the successors they have invested in to take the baton and carry on the mission of the organization. Every leader should be investing in future leaders and potential successors for their role. This includes teaching, training, being a mentor, and providing opportunities for others to develop their skills. Ultimately, who the successor will be and what type of succession system is in place is left up to the pastor or senior board leaders, depending on how your church is structured. This should be decided with much prayer, as success of the church depends on it.

CHAPTER 22

Methods for Leader Development

THERE ARE NUMEROUS approaches for leadership development, and we have identified several. The focus is on learning and continual development coming from various avenues such as life experiences, training, and the like. In this section, we pull it all together to highlight key approaches to leader development. Some of them, such as discipleship, are more familiar to churches than others, like coaching and assessments. Thus, we briefly compare and contrast those topics and delve a little deeper into the less familiar in regard to how they can be applicable to the church. Some of the main leader development methods include: 360 assessments, mentoring, discipleship, and coaching. Pastors and other leaders will also often use counseling or bring in a consultant, so these are included for clarification of roles.

360 Assessments

Every leader should take time to assess their current perspective and how it aligns with the perspective of their followers. This is precisely what 360-degree feedback assessments are designed to accomplish. 360-degree assessments are similar to self-assessments except they include the perspective of others as well. They can be formal or informal instruments that are commercially available for use in organizations or custom-designed assessments based on competencies the organization deems necessary for success. The 360 feedback process collects feedback that is used for personal and professional development. 360-degree assessments can provide specific areas for goal setting when connecting to real situations the leader is facing, creating an opportunity for changing perceptions and behavior.[45] The leader can use this information to develop, and a coach can assist the leader in exploring new insights, which can help focus the leader on how to be more successful.

Comparison of Approaches

Counseling, discipleship, and mentoring are some of the most familiar approaches utilized in churches. Coaching is a less familiar concept, and thus we explore and compare it to other methods in more detail in hopes of bringing a new approach to leader development in churches (please see Appendix A). Counseling focuses more on helping people get well, while coaching works with "healthy" people who want to develop or improve their lives.[46] Mentoring typically involves a more senior individual imparting wisdom, counsel, or opportunities to a more junior person,[47] whereas coaching draws out the abilities God has put in that person. In other words, coaching is helping the person learn through their own insights instead of teaching them new methods.[48] Discipleship is more focused than mentoring or coaching, as it centers on teaching biblical truths and spiritual development that allows people to grow in Christ.[49] Consulting involves analyzing a situation and giving expert advice, while coaching does not involve giving expert advice or solutions, instead involving listening, asking insightful questions, and guiding a person to make his or her own decisions and then take action to reach those goals.[50] The following table provides a further comparison of these approaches.[51,52]

Coaching	Counseling	Mentoring	Discipleship	Consulting
Focuses on helping people learn through their own God-given abilities and resources	Focuses on overcoming problems, conflicts, etc.	Focuses on teaching people	Focuses on teaching biblical truths for spiritual development	Focuses on providing expertise and solutions to issues
Enables people to reach goals, stimulates to make their own decisions and judgments	Diagnosis and fixes what is wrong; provides expertise, advice and strategies to solve issues	Imparts wisdom, counsel, and opportunities to junior person	Provides instruction and guidance	Emphasis on imparting information through instruction and tutoring
Focuses on present and future possibilities (e.g. getting unstuck; reaching goals)	Focuses on causes of issues from the past and bringing stability and healing	Uses support and accountability to develop people toward a better future	May use various methodologies: coaching, mentoring, or counseling to help Christians grow	Analyze existing practices and problems; suggests improvements for future development

We highly recommend using a combination of methods to develop leaders within the church. The Appendices provide further information on how to incorporate coaching and consulting into your leader development program.

Activity

As anonymous 360-degree feedback, have at least two other people who know you well complete the following assessments found in Appendices B, C, and D: Servant Leadership, Transformational, and Communication. You should still have your scores from Module 2. Compare their results with your original scores.

Conclusion

Leadership is a crucial topic in the church for individual development and overall church growth. While this was not intended to be a comprehensive study featuring an exhaustive list of leadership theory and practice, we have identified three cords of leadership that are vital to the growth process. All three cords—spiritual formation, leadership, and organizational development—when woven together, will make a strong and vibrant church body. We pray you will continue to develop as leaders for the cause of Christ. We want to congratulate you for finishing the study! Thank you for your support and dedication to God.

Module 3 Notes

1 Richard. L. Hughes and Katherine M. Beatty, *Becoming a Strategic Leader: Your Role in Your Organization's Enduring Success* (San Francisco: Jossey-Bass, 2005), 19–33.

2 Balanced Score Card Institute, "Strategic Planning Basics," 2014, https://balancedscorecard.

3 Fran Ackermann and Colin Eden, *Making Strategy: Mapping Out Strategic Success*, 2nd ed. (Thousand Oaks, CA: SAGE Publications, 2011), 14–34.

4 William E. Schneider, "Why good management ideas fail: The neglected power of organizational culture," *Strategy & Leadership* 28, no.1 (January, 2000), 24–29, doi:10.1108/10878570010336001.

5 Hughes and Beatty, *Becoming a Strategic Leader*, 53–82.

6 Andrew J. Dubrin, *Fundamentals of Organizational Behavior*, 4th ed. (Mason, OH: Cengage Learning, 2007), 336–344.

7 Debra L. Nelson and James Campbell Quick, *ORGB 3*, 3rd ed. (Mason, OH: South-Western, 2013), 262–278.

8 Edgar H. Schein, *Organizational Culture and Leadership*, 4th ed. (San Francisco: Jossey-Bass, 2010), 237–250.

9 Dubrin, *Fundamentals of Organizational Behavior*, 336–351.

10 James Kouzes and Barry Posner, *The Leadership Challenge: How to Make Extraordinary Things Happen in Organizations*, (San Francisco: Jossey-Bass, 2012), 41–71.

11 Dubrin, *Fundamentals of Organizational Behavior*, 336–351.

12 Kim S. Cameron and Robert E. Quinn, *Diagnosing and Changing Organizational Culture: Based on the Competing Values Framework* (San Francisco: Jossey-Bass, 2011), 27–35.

13 Jeffrey Pfeffer and Robert I. Sutton, *The Knowing-Doing Gap: How Smart Companies Turn Knowledge into Action* (Boston: Harvard Business School Publishing, 2000).

14 Jeffrey E. Haymond, "The Proverbs 31 Woman: Entrepreneurial Epitome?" *Faith & Economics* 60 (Fall 2012): 1–16. http://digitalcommons.cedarville.edu/cgi/viewcontent.cgi?article=1041&context=business_administration_publications.

15 Stuart E. Lucas, "The Power and Purpose of Entrepreneurial Stewardship," in *Wealth: Grow It and Protect It* (Upper Saddle River, NJ: Financial Times Press, 2012). http://www.ftpress.com/articles/article.aspx?p=2005112&seqNum=12.

16 John B. McGuire, Charles J. Palus, William Pasmore, and Gary B. Rhodes, "Transforming Your Organization: Global Organizational Development White Paper Series," Center for Creative Leadership, 2009. Accessed June 2, 2015, http://insights.ccl.org/wp-content/uploads/2015/04/TYO.pdf.

17 David A. Garvin, Amy C. Edmonson, and Francesca Gino, "Is Yours a Learning Organization?" *Harvard Business Review* (March, 2008). Accessed June 3, 2015, http://hbr.org/2008/03/is-yours-a-learning-organization/ar/1.

18 Josh Bersin, "5 Keys to Building a Learning Organization," *Forbes* (blog), January 18, 2012. Accessed June 3, 2015, http://www.forbes.com/sites/joshbersin/2012/01/18/5-keys-to-building-a-learning-organization/2/.

19 Chambers and Associates, "Developing a Culture of Leadership: A Systems Based Approach to Leadership Development," 2015. http://www.chambersandassociates.ca/pdf/Developing%20a%20Culture%20of%20Leadership.pdf.

20 Zeynep Aycan, "Leadership and Teamwork in Developing Countries: Challenges and Opportunities," *Online Readings in Psychology and Culture*, 7, no. 2. doi:10.9707/2307-0919.1066.

21 Manfred W. Kohl, "Radical Change is Required for the Leadership of the Church Today 'Let's Get Back to Basics,'" *International Congregational Journal* 6, no. 2 (2007), 113–118. http://0-eds.a.ebscohost.com.library.regent.edu/ehost/pdfviewer/pdfviewer?vid=2&sid=1a90631f-1585-40be-9b3f-989cd5e13da7%40sessionmgr4002&hid=4202.

22 Alister E. McGrath, *The Future of Christianity* (Malden, MA: Blackwell Publishers, 2002), 77–114.

23 Brian Davis, *Retention 101: A Practical Guide for Keeping More People* (Davis Media, 2011).

24 Amy L. Kristof-Brown, Ryan D. Zimmerman, and Erin C. Johnson, "Consequences of Individuals' Fit at Work: A Meta-Analysis of Person–Job, Person–Organization, Person–Group, and Person–Supervisor Fit," *Personnel Psychology* 58, no. 2 (June, 2005), 281–342. doi:10.1111/j.1744-6570.2005.00672.x.

25 Peter G. Northouse, *Leadership: Theory and Practice*, 6th ed. (Thousand Oaks, CA: SAGE Publications, Inc., 2013), 253–281.

26 John J. Sullivan, *Servant First! Leadership for the New Millennium* (Maitland, FL: Xulon Press, 2004), 107–142.

27 Mike Losey, Sue Meisinger, and Dave Ulrich, *The Future of Human Resource Management: 64 Thought Leaders Explore the Critical HR Issues of Today and Tomorrow* (Hoboken, NJ: John Wiley & Sons, Inc., 2005), 46–51.

28 J. Richard Hackman, *Leading Teams: Setting the Stage for Great Performances* (Boston, MA: Harvard Business School Press, 2002), 23–31.

29 Adam Canwell, Vishalli Dongrie, Neil Neveras, and Heather Stockton, "Developing 21st-Century Leadership Skills," *Mworld* 13, no. 3 (September, 2014), 38–43. http://0-eds.a.ebscohost.com.library.regent.edu/eds/pdfviewer/pdfviewer?sid=b9592383-a504-4c0e-a4ba-5919d2844960%40sessionmgr4001&vid=4&hid=4102.

30 Lee Gardenswartz, Anita Rowe, Patricia Digh, Martin Bennett, *The Global Diversity Desk Reference: Managing an International Workforce* (San Francisco: John Wiley & Sons, Inc., 2003), 139–154.

31 Hackman, *Leading Teams,* 200–232.

32 Dubrin, *Fundamentals of Organizational Behavior,* 189.

33 Hackman, *Leading Teams,* 30–33.

34 Ellen Van Velsor, Cynthia D. McCauley, and Marian N. Ruderman, eds., *The Center for Creative Leadership Handbook of Leadership Development*, 3rd ed. (San Francisco: Jossey-Bass, 2010).

35 Richard M. Burton, Børge Obel, and Gerardine DeSanctis. *Organizational Design: A Step-By-Step Approach*, 2nd ed. (Cambridge: Cambridge University Press, 2006).

36 Cynthia D. McCauley, Kim Kanaga, and Kim Lafferty, "Leader Development Systems," in *The Center for Creative Leadership Handbook of Leadership Development*, 3rd ed., eds. Ellen Van Velsor, Cynthia D. McCauley, and Marian N. Ruderman (San Francisco: Jossey-Bass, 2010), 29–62.

37 Vijayan P. Munusamy, Marian N. Ruderman, Regina H. Eckert, "Leader Development and Social Identity," in *The Center for Creative Leadership Handbook of*

Leadership Development, 3rd ed., eds. Ellen Van Velsor, Cynthia D. McCauley, and Marian N. Ruderman (San Francisco: Jossey-Bass, 2010), 147–176.

38 Ibid.

39 Ibid.

40 Ibid.

41 Cameron and Quinn, *Diagnosing and Changing Organizational Culture*, 27–35.

42 McCauley, Kanaga, and Lafferty, "Leader Development Systems," 2010.

43 William J. Rothwell, *Effective Succession Planning: Ensuring Leadership Continuity and Building Talent from Within*, 3rd ed. (New York, NY: American Management Association, 2005), 35–40.

44 Jeremy Lang, *From One Timothy to Another: A Guide for the Aspiring Minister* (Mizoram, India: Omega Arts & Offset Printing, 2008).

45 Nick Wright, "Gestalt meets cognitive behavioral coaching," *Training Journal* 64, (January, 2012). http://www.nick-wright.com/gestalt-meets-cognitive-coaching.html.

46 Tony Stoltzfus, *Leadership Coaching: The Disciplines, Skills, and Heart of a Christian Coach*, (Virginia Beach, VA: Tony Stoltzfus, 2005), 14.

47 Ibid., 10.

48 Collins, *Christian Coaching*, 157.

49 Ibid., 174.

50 Ibid., 132-139.

51 Ibid.

52 Stoltzfus, *Leadership Coaching*, 2005.

Coaching Techniques for Leaders

LEADERSHIP DEVELOPMENT IS vital to the success of any organization. Although there are many resources to help organizations develop their leadership talent, coaching has been a successful tool for helping both individuals and organizations reach their goals. There is significant research providing evidence that indicates leaders who are effective at coaching their employees achieve superior business results.[1] In fact, the Center for Creative Leadership (CCL) describes coaching as leading, because leaders with coaching skills are able to motivate work that enhances relationships and productivity.[2] Coaching as a leadership development option has many organizational benefits, including increased leadership skills and competencies, productivity, communication, relationships, and return on investment. Thus, coaching is an effective means to assist leaders in reaching their fullest potential and to then impart that growth to followers in any organization, including the church.

Those organizations wanting to experience the value of coaching may hire an external coach or have an internal coach on staff, but either way, coaching will help develop leaders. A successful coaching initiative will not only meet the needs of the individual but also the needs of the organization. The key for success is to ensure the coaching initiative aligns with organizational strategy and that there is strong support, clear boundaries, integration with processes, and a way to evaluate accomplishments. Organizations that invest in developing their leaders through coaching will see the value and return through organizational growth and success.

There are numerous scriptures that challenge the believer to continue to grow and develop. The talents parable in Matthew 25:15–46 is a good example, demonstrating the importance of development. In this pericope, Jesus called the servant wicked because he did not grow or develop the talent he was given. Additional scriptures that discuss growth and development include Ephesians 4:14–15, 2 Peter 3:18, Philippians 1:9, and 2 Peter 3:18. Coaching aligns with these biblical principles, as coaches are change agents who help people act to maximize their own potential and take responsibility for their lives.[3]

Despite our awareness of scripture concerning the importance of development, there is a tremendous need for leadership development in the church today. Many churches face a decline in attendance, which directly affects what leaders are available and willing to take on ministry roles.[4] There are numerous reasons for this, including a postmodern society, unrealistic expectations, untapped potential, systems not geared toward adult learning, and lack of leadership.[5] Furthermore, there is an instinctive longing for authentic relationships and a sense of self-understanding, identity, direction, and clarity of purpose in today's culture.[6] Thus, the church must aggressively respond to these needs by focusing on leadership training and development. Coaching is a great approach for working toward meeting these needs, as it focuses on relationships, self-awareness, and development. In fact, several studies have found that coaching is an effective method for leadership development, and is not only effective for individuals but also ministry teams in Christian organizations.[7,8] Coaching in ministry can help to develop leaders, reach goals, find clarity and focus, cultivate strengths, instill confidence, and foster learning and progress, along with numerous other benefits.[9]

Some church members may already be trained as coaches. These members can be instrumental in incorporating a coaching initiative. While everyone is not a trained coach, there are some coaching skills for developing others that all leaders can improve and incorporate into their skill set. These include: listening, building relationships, asking insightful questions, and empowering.[10]

Listen: Listening is a necessary skill for both effective coaching and leadership, but is a trait that many leaders might need to develop. We have all seen leaders who are good at leading people or doing what they are put in position to do, but lack in communication skills such as truly listening to their followers. Often, leaders have so much knowledge to share with followers that they may do more talking than listening. However, the Bible teaches it is better to listen than to speak too quickly: be slow to speak and quick to hear (James 1:19). Listening is one of the most important actions of a leader, as it helps to build strength in people.

Build Relationships: Establishing a relationship is one of the best ways to lead and coach a person. It builds trust, rapport, and empathy. Building relationships takes time, but as people get to know one another, they begin to feel safer opening up and revealing more about themselves. Leaders who cultivate relationships are more apt to successfully help someone grow. This also applies to discipleship and has been one of the most effective strategies of outreach. How we interact with and respond to people will either build up or destroy leader–follower relationships. Thus, it is important to communicate effectively, not judge, and have the fruit and gifts of the Spirit working through us (Galatians 5:22–23; 1 Corinthians 12:8–10).

Ask Insightful Questions: Coaches ask thought-provoking questions to promote and provoke insight, action, and discovery.[11] They help people determine goals and then develop strategies to obtain these goals. Instead of telling people the answer, as consultants would do, coaches enhance development by aiding people in the discovery process. Most people know themselves and what they want, but there are things that sabotage their progress. Coaches can ask probing questions to help reveal desires and uncover what is inhibiting progress. Closed questions such as those that require only a yes or no answer do not facilitate this type of discovery, but open questions provide insight needed to move forward. For example, a person may ask, "Do you have any options?" (closed question). The person would respond with a yes, no, or maybe. Whereas, an open question is "What are your options?" This question compels the person to identify what options there are and to think through possibilities.

Empower: Coaching not only recognizes that people can achieve more than they might have imagined, but also empowers people by helping them set their own goals and agendas, then holding them accountable. Coaches guide people to make their own decisions and take actions to reach their goals. They believe in people in order to empower them to change. Effective apostolic leaders should be authentic, to gain trust and credibility with followers, as well as empower them to develop their own sense of self, authenticity, and leadership skills.

There are many other coaching competencies that go deeper in helping a person move forward and develop, but that is outside of the scope of this book. These basic skills will allow leaders to coach followers instead of giving them answers to their issues. This, combined with discipleship and mentoring, will enhance the growth process.

Consulting

Consultants are professionals who give expert advice to individuals and organizations in order to help resolve issues and reach desired goals.[12,13] Their assistance may come in the form of recommendations, information, or actual hands-on work.[14] Consultants bring fresh new ideas and perspectives to organizations, leading to optimal performance.[15] Some advantages of hiring a consultant include:

- **Providing Advice and Expert Solutions to Individual or Organizational Challenges**. Hiring a consultant has the benefit of introducing skills and abilities not available in your organization. They can enhance productivity, providing results within a specified time.[16] Consultants bring expertise that helps solve problems more effectively and efficiently.

- **Supplying an Outside Perspective**. It is possible to be too close to an issue, resulting in an inability to see things clearly in order to resolve challenges. A consultant brings much-needed objectivity by providing fresh eyes to a situation, without preconceived notions that internal people may have. This objective viewpoint can help resolve politics and find solutions to operational or technical problems that commonly cloud and complicate issues. Yes, unfortunately, politics do sometimes exist in the church. Consultants also ensure credibility, as some leaders perceive the opinion of the "expert" as the only one that counts.

- **Filling Needed Gaps**. Many organizations have needs requiring skills or resources that are not available in-house or that staff do not have time to address. Consultants can help meet that need by asking the right questions, providing solutions, and alleviating perceived constraints. This will enable internal staff to be fully present in their jobs, such as strategic planning meetings, where leaders frequently must coordinate, facilitate, and participate.

- **Offering Cost Savings**. Consultants can handle tasks on a short-term basis and do not stay on payroll once the project is complete, like regular employees. This saves on a church's administrative costs, benefits, and payroll. Additionally, consultants are more likely to correctly complete projects in a shorter amount of time, cutting costs for training and avoiding expensive pitfalls.

Appendix A Notes

1 James M. Hunt and Joseph R. Weintraub, *The Coaching Organization: A Strategy for Developing Leaders* (Thousand Oaks, CA: Sage Publications, 2007).

2 Center for Creative Leadership, "Coaching Skills Development," Center for Creative Leadership (CCL), 2015. http://www.ccl.org/leadership/coaching/skills.aspx.

3 Stoltzfus, *Leadership Coaching,* 6.

4 Jane Creswell, *Christ-Centered Coaching: 7 Benefits for Ministry Leaders* (Danvers, MA: Chalice Press, 2006), 2. Accessed June 2, 2014, http://books.google.com/book s?hl=en&lr=&id=1oqZy4Vy7ScC&oi=fnd&pg=PR8&dq=coaching+in+ministry&ots =ygHz5jsNHo&sig=mVCQ78GrFNA2mMDGjHvv8HxaTx8#v=onepage&q=coachi ng%20in%20ministry&f=false.

5 Brian Simon, "A Responsive Coaching Model for Transformational Training of Emerging Postmodern Church Leadership," (doctorate thesis, Regent University, 2006), 12–14. Accessed May 30, 2014, http://0-search.proquest.com.library.regent. edu/pqdtlocal1006574/docview/304924694/9D12D831E22B4BDFPQ/2?account id=13479.

6 Ibid., 14.

7 Kenneth O. Gangel, *Coaching Ministry Teams: Leadership and Management in Christian Organizations* (Eugene, OR: Wipf and Stock Publishers, 2006), 1–4. http:// books.google.com/books?hl=en&lr=&id=2JJLAwAAQBAJ&oi=fnd&pg=PR9&dq=coa ching+in+ministry&ots=P-y0K-LT83&sig=aHyqOqOHNZZ4Su2bEIkwQO1jWoU# v=onepage&q=coaching%20in%20ministry&f=false.

8 Ibid., 19.

9 Creswell, *Christ-Centered Coaching,* 5–9.

10 Ibid., 132–139.

11 Hunt and Weintraub, *The Coaching Organization,* 283.

12 Linda K. Stroh and Homer H. Johnson. *The Basic Principles of Effective Consulting* (Mahwah, NJ: Lawrence Erlbaum Associates, 2006).

13 USDA Office of Human Resources Management Virtual University, "Differences Between Coaching, Counseling, Managing, Mentoring, Consulting, and Training," USDA Virtual University, last modified August 28, 2014, http://www.dm.usda.gov/ employ/vu/coaching-diff.htm.

14 Elaine Biech, *The Business of Consulting: The Basics and Beyond,* 2nd ed. (San Francisco: John Wiley & Sons, 2007), 1–2.

15 Ron Pickard, "Why hire a consultant?" RPQ Consulting. Accessed August 19, 2014, http://www.rpqconsulting.com/Why_Hire_a_Consultant.pdf (site discontinued).

16 Jack Gordon, "Advantages & Disadvantages of Hiring a Consultant," eHow, last modified May 18, 2014, http://www.ehow.com/info_8248009_advantages-disadvan-tages-hiring-consultant.html.

Servant Leadership Assessment

INSTRUCTIONS: USING THE following 5-point scale, indicate the extent to which you agree or disagree with the following statements as they pertain to your leadership.

Note: This questionnaire can also be completed as a 360-degree assessment by replacing the words "you" with "he/she" and having at least two people rate the extent to which they agree or disagree with the following statements concerning your leadership.

Key:　1 = Strongly Disagree　　2 = Disagree　　3 = Neutral
　　　　　4 = Agree　　　　　　　5 = Strongly Agree

1. Others seek help from you if they have personal problems.　　　　　　　　　　　　1 2 3 4 5
2. You emphasize the importance of giving back to the community.　　　　　　　　　　1 2 3 4 5
3. You can tell if something is going wrong and how to avoid problems.　　　　　　　1 2 3 4 5

4. You give others the responsibility to make important decisions about their duties. 1 2 3 4 5

5. You carefully listen to others' needs. 1 2 3 4 5

6. You care more about being real with people than you do status. 1 2 3 4 5

7. You hold high ethical standards. 1 2 3 4 5

8. You are interested in making sure others' needs are taken care of. 1 2 3 4 5

9. You love and care about others' personal well-being. 1 2 3 4 5

10. Others trust you with confidential information. 1 2 3 4 5

11. You are able to think through complex issues. 1 2 3 4 5

12. You are always interested in helping people in the church/community. 1 2 3 4 5

13. You help people discover their potential and obtain their goals. 1 2 3 4 5

14. You are always honest. 1 2 3 4 5

15. You take time to talk to others on a personal level. 1 2 3 4 5

16. You are involved in church/community activities. 1 2 3 4 5

17. You have a thorough understanding of the church and its goals. 1 2 3 4 5

18. You give others the freedom to handle difficult situations in the way they feel is best. 1 2 3 4 5

19. You provide others with tasks and experiences that enable them to develop new skills. 1 2 3 4 5

20. You sacrifice your own interests to meet others' needs. 1 2 3 4 5

21. You would not compromise ethical principles in order to meet a goal or reach success. 1 2 3 4 5

22. You encourage others to volunteer in the church/ community. 1 2 3 4 5

23. You can recognize when others are feeling down without asking them. 1 2 3 4 5

24. You can solve issues with new or creative ideas. 1 2 3 4 5

25. You want to understand others' perspectives. 1 2 3 4 5

26. You are aware of and able to see potential threats to individuals and the group as a whole. 1 2 3 4 5

27. The way others view your character is important to you. 1 2 3 4 5

28. You value honesty more than achievements. 1 2 3 4 5

29. You are aware of others' situation and how it may affect their future. 1 2 3 4 5

30. You treat others as you want to be treated and help them unselfishly. 1 2 3 4 5

31. You demonstrate ethical conduct in every decision. 1 2 3 4 5

32. You do not seek recognition. 1 2 3 4 5

33. You have clear and consistent communication that convinces people to change when necessary. 1 2 3 4 5

34. You know that God is in control but you must do your part. 1 2 3 4 5

35. You are who you say you are. 1 2 3 4 5

36. You do not use your power of influence to manipulate. 1 2 3 4 5

Scoring: Add up your total score for each category using the key below, then see Scoring Interpretation. For the 360-degree feedback scores, average the totals for each question and use that to reference Scoring Interpretation. For example, if you had two other people provide feedback and one scored a 3 for question #1 and the other rated a 5, then your average for question #1 is 4. Add all averages to get your total 360-degree feedback score.

1. Add up scores on 1, 8, 9, 12, 15, 20, 25, 30, and 32. This is your score for Love: humility, empathy, altruism, healing, and service.
2. Add up scores on 3, 5, 11, 17, 23, 24, 26, 29, and 34. This is your score for Discernment: awareness, internal locus of control, listening, conceptualization, and foresight.
3. Add up scores on 2, 4, 13, 16, 18, 19, 22, 33, and 36. This is your score for Stewardship: growth, persuasion, community, and empowerment.
4. Add up scores on 6, 7, 10,14, 21, 27, 28, 31, and 35. This is your score for Integrity: authenticity, ethics, trust, and honor.

Scoring Interpretation

High range: A score between 31 and 45 means you strongly exhibit this servant leadership characteristic.
Moderate range: A score between 16 and 30 means you exhibit this characteristic in an average way.

Low range: A score between 0 and 15 means you exhibit this servant leadership characteristic below the average or expected degree.

The scores received on the Servant Leadership Questionnaire indicate the degree to which you exhibit each of the four constructs from the servant leader model. Use the results to evaluate what areas you are strong in and which ones you may want to strive to improve.

Transformational Assessment

INSTRUCTIONS: USING THE following 4-point scale, indicate to what degree you utilize each of the following statements in your leadership style.

Note: This questionnaire can also be completed as a 360-degree assessment by replacing the words "I" with "he/she" and having at least two people rate the extent to which they feel you utilize each of the statements in your leadership. Then compare these to your own scores.

Key: 0 = Not at all   1 = Once in a while   2 = Sometimes
           3 = Fairly often   4 = Frequently, if not always

1. I help people find and develop their strengths.   0 1 2 3 4
2. I create a shared vision.   0 1 2 3 4
3. I consider consequences before making decisions, taking into consideration morality and ethics.   0 1 2 3 4
4. I consider the group before my own self-interests.   0 1 2 3 4
5. I speak positively about future outcomes.   0 1 2 3 4

6. I am able to motivate followers to go beyond
their own interests for the good of the church
and society.   0 1 2 3 4

7. I scrutinize the status quo to question whether
it is appropriate.   0 1 2 3 4

8. I understand what and when something needs
to change in order to reach our goals, and then
I model the way.   0 1 2 3 4

Scoring: Add up the total of your answers, then see Scoring Interpretation.

Scoring Interpretation

High range: A score between 22 and 32 means you strongly exhibit transformational leadership characteristics.

Moderate range: A score between 11 and 21 means you exhibit transformational leadership characteristics in an average way.

Low range: A score between 0 and 10 means you exhibit transformational leadership characteristics below the average or expected degree.

The scores received on the Transformational Questionnaire indicate the degree to which you exhibit transformational leadership characteristics. Use the results to evaluate what areas you are strong in and which ones you may want to strive to improve.

Communication Assessment

INSTRUCTIONS: SELECT THE response that best describes the frequency of your actual behavior.

Note: This questionnaire can also be completed as a 360-degree assessment by replacing the words "I" with "he/she" and having at least two people rate the extent to which they agree or disagree with the following statements concerning your leadership. Then compare these to your own scores.

Key: 0 = Not at all   1 = Seldom   2 = Occasionally

3 = Frequently   4 = Usually   5 = Almost always

1. I show others I enjoy listening to them speak by demonstratinginterest, nodding, smiling, and so forth.   0 1 2 3 4 5

2. I try not to pay closer attention to people who are more similar to me than people who are different from me.   0 1 2 3 4 5

3. I speak clearly and use words the other person can understand.   0 1 2 3 4 5

4. I assess people's verbal and nonverbal communication.   0 1 2 3 4 5

5. When people are talking, I allow them time to finish; I do not interrupt, anticipate what they are saying, or jump to conclusions.   0 1 2 3 4 5

6. I understand that people come from diverse backgrounds and consider this in my communications with them.   0 1 2 3 4 5

7. I do not think about what I am going to say next when the other person is talking.   0 1 2 3 4 5

8. When I don't understand something, I let the other person know and ask direct questions to get the person to further explain.   0 1 2 3 4 5

9. When listening to other people, I try to see things from their perspective.   0 1 2 3 4 5

10. I do not repeat myself but concisely say what I intend to say.   0 1 2 3 4 5

11. I learn about a person's culture in order to be sensitive and effectively communicate with them.   0 1 2 3 4 5

12. I pay attention to my body language and words to ensure that I am communicating what I intend.   0 1 2 3 4 5

13. I pay attention when someone is speaking to me and do not allow myself to get easily distracted.   0 1 2 3 4 5

14. I let the other person know that I understand what he or she is saying by restating their comments in my own words.   0 1 2 3 4 5

15. I try to put myself in others' shoes to better relate to and understand their position. 0 1 2 3 4 5

16. I purposely connect with people of different cultures, origins, and backgrounds in order to broaden my perspective. 0 1 2 3 4 5

17. I understand how to accurately interpret subtle gestures of body language such as facial expressions and hand movements. 0 1 2 3 4 5

18. I know that I do not always have to agree in order to understand how a person feels and why. 0 1 2 3 4 5

19. I am aware of my posture, eye contact, and demeanor and how it affects my leadership ability. 0 1 2 3 4 5

20. I strive to allow the love of God to shine through me even in my communication. 0 1 2 3 4 5

Scoring: Add up your total score for each category using the key below, then see Scoring Interpretation. There is a total of 100 points, 20 points for each category. The following numbers correspond with specific communication skills:

1. Add up scores on 1, 5, 7, and 13. This is your score for Listening.

2. Add up scores on 3, 8, 10, and 14. This is your score for Speaking.

3. Add up scores on 2, 6, 11, and 16. This is your score for Diversity.

4. Add up scores on 9, 15, 18, and 20. This is your score for Empathy.

5. Add up scores on 4, 12, 17, and 19. This is your score for Nonverbal.

Scoring Interpretation

High range: A score between 14 and 20 means you strongly exhibit this communication skill.

Moderate range: A score between 7 and 13 means you exhibit this communication skill in an average way.

Low range: A score between 0 and 6 means you exhibit this communication skill below the average or expected degree.

The scores received on the Communication Assessment indicate the degree to which you exhibit each of the five communication skills. Use the results to evaluate what areas you are strong in and which ones you may want to strive to improve.

About the Authors

DR. AMY OLSON has served in leadership and ministry roles at congregations of all sizes for more than twenty years, and has over fifteen years experience in organizational leadership and management. Amy obtained her doctorate in strategic leadership from Regent University's School of Business and Leadership, and is an internationally published author, professor, strategic advisor and executive coach. In addition to her passion for developing Christian leaders and teams, Amy enjoys playing music, traveling, and spending time with her family.

Chris Olson is an ordained minister who has served in leadership and ministry roles at congregations of all sizes for nearly twenty years. He has more than fifteen years experience in business management and organizational leadership. Chris has a master's degree in organizational leadership with a concentration in organizational development consulting from Regent University's School of Business and Leadership. Additionally, he is a published author, professor, and leadership consultant. His passion lies in teaching and developing systems and process for Christian leaders.

Amy and Chris Olson are the founders of the
Center for Apostolic Leadership.
www.apostolicleader.org

Made in the USA
Coppell, TX
15 April 2020

19968279R00142